CONTENTS

Chapter One: Overview

Chapter Two: Young People and Crime

Chapter Three: Crime Prevention

Introduction

Dealing with Crime is the eighty-third volume in the **Issues** series. The aim of this series is to offer up-to-date information about important issues in our world.

Dealing with Crime looks at trends in crime, young people and crime and crime prevention.

The information comes from a wide variety of sources and includes:
Government reports and statistics
Newspaper reports and features
Magazine articles and surveys
Web site material
Literature from lobby groups
and charitable organisations.

It is hoped that, as you read about the many aspects of the issues explored in this book, you will critically evaluate the information presented. It is important that you decide whether you are being presented with facts or opinions. Does the writer give a biased or an unbiased report? If an opinion is being expressed, do you agree with the writer?

Dealing with Crime offers a useful starting-point for those who need convenient access to information about the many issues involved. However, it is only a starting-point. At the back of the book is a list of organisations which you may want to contact for further information.

*****

Dealing with Crime

ISSUES

Volume 83

Editor

Craig Donnellan

Independence

Educational Publishers

First published by Independence
PO Box 295
Cambridge CB1 3XP
England

© Craig Donnellan 2004

British Library Cataloguing in Publication Data
Dealing with Crime – (Issues Series)
I. Donnellan, Craig II. Series
364

ISBN 1 86168 278 6

Printed in Great Britain
MWL Print Group Ltd

Typeset by
Claire Boyd

Cover
The illustration on the front cover is by
Pumpkin House.

Crime and justice

Information from *Social Trends*

Crime, in some form, affects many people during their lives. Dealing with crime and its impact is a continual problem for both society and government. The Government's current priorities include tackling street crime, introducing changes in the handling of drug offences and reforming the criminal justice system.

Crime rates

There are difficulties in determining the true level of crime in this country. Two main measures are used, each with its own strengths and weaknesses. One measure is the amount of crime recorded by the police, and the other comes from surveys of victims, including the *British Crime Survey* (BCS). The table on page two gives more details on these two measures of crime.

From recorded crime figures for England and Wales, it is estimated that in 2001/02 there was a 2 per cent increase in the underlying crime trend compared with the previous year. Although the 5.5 million crimes recorded by the police in 2001/02 were 7 per cent more than the previous financial year, a substantial part of this increase is likely to be due to the changes in the methods and rules for the recording of crime. These were estimated to have inflated the number of crimes recorded in 2001/02 by 5 per cent.

Crime in Scotland showed little overall change between 2000 and 2001, with a total of 421,000 crimes recorded by the police. In Scotland the term 'crimes' is used for the more serious criminal acts (roughly equivalent to 'indictable' and 'triable-either-way' offences in England and Wales). Less serious crimes are termed 'offences'.

Recorded crime in Northern Ireland increased by around 17 per cent between 2000/01 and 2001/02. A major factor behind this increase was the implementation of a new recording system which resulted in more low-level crime being recorded. In Northern Ireland the definitions used are broadly comparable with those in England and Wales.

After taking into account changes in the recording of crimes, there were rises in certain types of crime recorded by the police in England and Wales, most notably robbery, which increased by 27 per cent between 2000/01 and 2001/02. Non-vehicle thefts increased by 6 per cent over the same period. Household burglary rose, after the adjustments, by 3 per cent and other burglary rose by 5 per cent. Violent crimes against the person fell by 5 per cent, after adjusting for the

---

Theft comprised almost half of all BCS crime in the 12 months prior to interview in 2001/02

---

recording changes, while sexual offences fell by 8 per cent. Theft and handling stolen goods accounted for around two-fifths of all crimes recorded in 2001/02, around the same proportion as in the previous year.

The *British Crime Survey* estimated that just over 13 million crimes occurred in England and Wales, based on interviews taking place in the 2001/02 financial year (covering crimes occurring in the twelve months prior to interview), a decrease of 14 per cent compared with the estimate of crimes taking place in 1999. Within this, there were large falls in domestic burglary (23 per cent), vehicle thefts (14 per cent) and common assaults (24 per cent).

Theft (including vehicle and other household theft, but not including burglary) comprised almost half of all BCS crime in the 12 months prior to interview in 2001/02; with crimes against property (vandalism, vehicle vandalism and burglary) accounting for around 30 per cent of crimes, and the remaining percentage comprising offences against the person: wounding (5 per cent), mugging (3 per cent) and common assaults (14 per cent).

Over three-quarters of the incidents measured in the 2001/02 *British Crime Survey*, around 10 million crimes, are comparable with those recorded by police statistics. Over two-fifths of comparable crimes in England and Wales in the twelve months prior to 2001/02 were reported to the police. The proportion of crimes reported varies according to the type of offence. Reasons for not reporting crimes commonly include the perception on the part of the victim that the incident was too trivial, that the police could not do anything, or that the matter was dealt with privately. High proportions of vehicle thefts (52 per cent) are reported to the police as a formal record of the incident and are generally needed for insurance purposes. Lower proportions of incidents of vandalism (31 per cent) are reported to the police. Reporting rates have fallen since 1991, when nearly half of crimes were reported to the police.

Measures of crime

There are two main measures of crime: estimates from surveys of victims, such as the *British Crime Survey* (BCS), and from data collected by the police. Crime data collected by the police are a by-product of the administrative procedure of completing a record for crimes which they investigate. BCS data are collated by interviewing members of households. The survey measures all 'incidents' irrespective of whether they were reported to or recorded by the police.

Police recorded crime and BCS measured crime have a different coverage. Unlike crime data recorded by the police, the BCS is restricted to crimes against adults (aged 16 or over) living in private households and their property and does not include some types of crime (for example, fraud, murder and so-called victimless crimes).

Not all crimes will be recorded by the police. Between 2000/01 and 2001/02, only one in four crimes in England and Wales were recorded by the police (60 per cent of those reported to the police). The police may choose not to record a reported crime for a number of reasons. They

may consider that the report of a crime is mistaken, too trivial or that there is insufficient evidence. Alternatively, the victim may not wish the police to proceed. Recording rates also vary according to the type of offence, with 19 per cent of vandalism recorded by the police and 42 per cent of household burglaries.

Periodic surveys are carried out to compare crime in different countries. Making direct comparisons is complicated by a number of factors: laws are different across international boundaries, and methods of collecting crime data vary enormously from country to country, with some relying more on administrative data collected by the police and others relying more on surveys. For these reasons, international crime comparisons are invariably given in terms of percentage changes for each country rather than rates. When comparing 1996 with 2000, crime recorded by the police in England and Wales fell by 8 per cent compared with an average 1 per cent rise in EU countries. Recorded crime in Scotland fell by 6 per cent over the same period. Within the EU,

crime in Belgium rose by the highest proportion (17 per cent); an increase which is far below the large increases in crime in a number of east European countries, including Slovenia (84 per cent), Estonia (63 per cent) and Poland (41 per cent).

The incidence of crime varies between different types of areas. Rural areas tend to have lower rates than non-rural areas, although the pattern of offences is similar. For three offence categories: burglary, vehicle-related thefts and violence, crime rates per 10,000 population in rural areas in England and Wales in 1999 were between a half and two-thirds the crime rates in non-rural areas. Although rural crime did increase faster than non-rural crime in the mid-1980s and early 1990s, increases or decreases in crime in both types of areas have tended to follow national trends in more recent years.

■ The above information is from *Social Trends No. 33*: 2003 edition. For further information visit www.statistics.gov.uk

Recorded crime: by type of offence, 2001/02

	England & Wales	Scotland[1]	Thousands Northern Ireland
Theft and handling stolen goods	2,267	171	42
of which			
theft of vehicles	328	23	12
theft from vehicles	655	40	7
Criminal damage	1,064	95	40
Burglary	879	45	17
Violence against the person	650	20	26
Fraud and forgery	317	21	9
Drug offences	121	36	1
Robbery	121	4	2
Sexual offences	41	5	1
of which			
rape	10	1	0
Other offences[2]	65	25	1
All notifiable offences	5,527	421	140

1 Figures for Scotland refer to 2001.
2 In Northern Ireland includes 'offences against the state'. In Scotland excludes 'offending while on bail'.

Source: Home Office; Scottish Executive; Police Service of Northern Ireland.
Social Trends No. 33: 2003 edition, Crown copyright

Surge in reports of violent crime

The number of violent crimes reported in Britain during the third quarter of 2003 rose 14% compared with the same period the previous year, according to crime figures released by the Home Office 22 January 2004.

Violent offences against the person between July and September last year rose 17% period-on-period, a figure that included an 18% rise in more serious violence such as homicide and serious wounding, and an 8% rise in sexual offences.

There were 11,800 offences of serious violence in the period, while crimes involving less serious violence, such as minor woundings, harassment, common assault and the possession of weapons, rose from 203,800 offences to 238,000.

While reported violent crime rose during the quarter, statistics collected by the *British Crime Survey*, which include crime that is not reported to the police, suggest that violent crime fell 3% overall in the 12 months to September.

The figures cover a period when seven-year-old Toni-Ann Byfield was fatally shot in the back in north London, and 64-year-old Marian Bates was killed during a robbery at her Nottingham jewellery shop.

The Home Office suggested that the rise in violent crime was partly due to the continuing impact of changes in the way that police record offences.

Criminal damage also increased by 7% in the third quarter last year, while recorded robberies fell by 2%, house burglaries fell by 3% and thefts from vehicles fell 8%, compared with the same period in 2002.

Overall, recorded crime levels were stable, Home Office statisticians said. The Home Office also announced that, from 22 January 2004, offenders in possession of an illegal firearm would receive a mandatory five-year prison sentence.

By Jeremy Lennard

A breakdown of gun crime in the October data showed that total firearms offences in England and Wales increased by 2% in the past financial year.

This was less than one-tenth of the 34% increase seen the year before, leading Home Office officials to conclude that the increase in gun crime peaked in autumn 2002.

Within the overall gun crime figures, however, imitation weapons were used in 1,815 reported crimes, a leap of 46% on the previous year.

Violent offences against the person between July and September last year rose 17% period-on-period

Data showed that homicides rose by 21% to 1,045 in 2002-03, but this included 172 victims of serial killer Harold Shipman. Excluding Shipman's victims, the rise was 1%.

'It is important to put the increases in police recording of violent crime into context,' said the Home Office minister, Hazel Blears.

'Better police crime recording policies mean that local forces now have a clearer picture of crime in their area and that anti-social behaviour and low-level thuggery,

which are included in the violent crime figures, are more accurately recorded.

'We are also making significant progress in the fight against gun crime, and the rate of increase has slowed considerably.

'The five-year mandatory sentence for possession of a firearm, and the new offences of possession of an air weapon or imitation firearm in a public place, as well as the ban on high-powered air cartridge weapons, will deter offenders and punish the perpetrators.

'We are determined to drive down gun crime and this sends out a tough message that anyone flouting our gun laws will face a lengthy time in prison,' Ms Blears added. But Paul Cavadino, the chief executive of the National Association for the Care and Resettlement of Offenders, warned that the new sentencing policy was wide of the mark.

'Tough minimum sentences will have little effect on gun crime. We will only tackle it effectively by reducing the supply of illegal weapons and combating the macho glamorised gun culture which attracts young people to firearms,' he said.

Mr Cavadino also insisted that, in order to reduce violent crime, alcohol abuse had to be tackled.

'A high proportion of violence is alcohol-fuelled, ranging from fights around pubs and clubs to domestic homicides. We badly need a national alcohol strategy covering prevention, education and treatment facilities for problem drinkers,' he said.

Chris Fox, president of the Association of Chief Police Officers, welcomed the data from the Home Office.

'It is good news that reported crime generally is not rising, and in many categories continues to fall. However, the continued rise in reported violent crime remains an issue of particular concern,' he said.

Gun crime

A problem ready to explode. John Steele reports

Police were warned of a rise in indiscriminate, drug-fuelled violence two decades ago, but the response was muted.

Gun crime has been the most urgent and dangerous law and order problem facing police in Britain over the past three years.

Many in the police service have long feared that there would be a multiple shooting or killing of unarmed officers, who are often first at the scene of crimes involving men carrying guns.

A poll of Police Federation members earlier this year emphasised that, so far, rank-and-file police do not wish to be routinely armed.

But local polls among frontline officers in London and some other areas suggest much stronger support for an armed force in inner-city areas. Though forces employ specialist firearms squads, they are relatively small.

One of the most notorious recent shootings of officers was in 1993, when Pc Pat Dunne, an unarmed beat officer in south-west London, was shot and killed as he walked into the path of gunmen who had already killed another man.

There have, however, been a number of instances in which shots, including hails of automatic bullets, have been fired in the direction of officers or their vehicles.

Though gun crime accounts for a tiny proportion of overall crime – around 0.18 per cent of recorded offences for non-air weapons – the fight against firearms crime consumes vast police resources.

The widely held public perception that gun crime is a 'criminal versus criminal' affair has some justification. Many victims of shootings are involved in crime, particularly drugs.

However, firearms crime is increasingly driven by the indiscriminate and often drug-fuelled violence of a group of young men who do not care who gets in the way of their bullets.

They shoot victims in the street, in 'drive-by' attacks or in nightclubs, in an attempt to wage war on rival gangs or, simply, to revenge themselves for perceived 'disrespect'.

British bank robbers have always been ready to use guns. And newly arrived immigrant communities, such as the Turkish/Kosovans and Albanians, have brought with them criminal elements who readily resort to guns to settle disputes.

However, the most pressing gun issue in the past decade has involved 'black on black' violence among criminal groups in London, Birmingham, Manchester, Bristol and Nottingham and other cities, much of it linked to the trade in crack cocaine.

Governments and police chiefs cannot claim that the rise in gun crime was not predictable.

In the 1980s law enforcement figures in the US warned Britain that crack – the highly addictive derivative of cocaine that caused mayhem in American cities – would cross the Atlantic. However, heroin, which

---

Though gun crime accounts for a tiny proportion of overall crime the fight against firearms crime consumes vast police resources

---

was then linked to the spread of Aids, remained the top priority.

By the early 1990s, a number of senior officers in the Metropolitan Police were beginning to warn of the dangers of the Jamaican Yardie-style culture of cash, cars, cocaine and guns. Again, though, the police response was limited.

That culture is now well entrenched and a concern for police is that similar gun violence will emerge in other, non-black areas.

The historical trends in gun crimes are disturbing. In 1991, guns accounted for around eight per cent of homicides – 50 out of 623. In the year to April 2002, around 11.5 per cent of victims died from firearms – 96 out of 832.

After a dip in the mid-1990s, firearm crimes rose from 6,063 in 1996 to 7,362 five years later.

Between 1997 and 2002, gun robberies rose from 2,836 to 5,233 and incidents of violence against the person involving non-air weapons went up from 1,463 to 3,444.

There is, however, some bleak consolation – gun violence, and murders, could be a lot worse if the young British criminals could get hold of better weapons.

Experts agree that there is a shortage of high-quality military guns and ammunition. The gunmen use what they can afford, or obtain, and much of it is home-made and inefficient.

A day in the life of yob-culture Britain

A snapshot of yobbish Britain has uncovered for the first time the scale of the disorder blighting the lives of millions of people.

On one day in September 2003, 66,000 incidents of rowdiness, intimidation, littering, drunkenness, drug-taking and vandalism were reported to various public agencies – more than one every two seconds.

Over the year, this would translate into 16 million 'low-level' offences, costing an estimated £3.5 billion to deal with and clear up.

The figures were gathered in the first census of anti-social behaviour in England and Wales. They provided the backdrop for a renewed Government effort to get to grips with the problem, headed by the Prime Minister.

Mr Blair's high-profile policy launch in London was a tacit admission that five years after making a priority of tackling the 'yob culture', little had improved. Ministers are now asking local officials to act against the troublemakers or face the axe.

The census was taken on 10 September 2003, a mid-week day during school term that was likely to give a typical return. The police, local authorities and other agencies were instructed to count the number of incidents over a 24-hour period.

More than 1,500 organisations took part in the sweep to measure the extent of street drinking, begging, rowdiness, vandalism, intimidation, littering, noise, prostitution and other aspects of disorder that cause greatest offence.

The results indicated that one person in five perceived high levels of disorder in their area.

The highest number of reports was generated by people dropping litter or dumping rubbish, vandalism, rowdiness and nuisance behaviour. There were nearly 5,000 complaints about abandoned vehicles and more than 6,000 about drunkenness and drug taking.

*By Philip Johnston,
Home Affairs Editor*

Mr Blair's involvement in the strategy indicates how seriously the Government takes increasing public despondency over the country's slide into squalor and blight.

However, doubts were raised over whether the latest drive would be any more successful than the last which was spearheaded by the Crime and Disorder Act 1998, with campaigners denouncing the measures as 'political posturing' and 'gimmickry'. Since Labour took office, more than £8 billion has been spent on various initiatives, such as anti-social behaviour orders, child curfews and on-the-spot fines.

Two dozen new measures are now going through Parliament under the Anti-Social Behaviour Bill. They include making begging a recordable offence and subject to community penalties and removing housing benefit from tenants whose persistently bad behaviour makes their neighbours' lives a misery.

Mr Blair told a London conference: 'I want to make one very simple point. To the police, housing officers, local authorities – we've listened, we've given you the powers, and it's time to use them.'

He added: 'You've got new powers to deal with nuisance neighbours – use them. You've got new powers to deal with abandoned cars – use them. You've got new powers to give fixed penalty fines for anti-social behaviour, without going through a long court process – use them.'

At the same event, David Blunkett, the Home Secretary, launched a fierce attack on public agencies that appeared unwilling to take the necessary action to clean up neighbourhoods and bear down on low-level offending.

'They are paid by the community and they should be held to account by the community if they don't do their job on behalf of the community,' he said.

He also denounced the 1960s and 1970s 'garbage' that still held sway among some officials that they should be 'non-judgemental' about

One day of anti-social behaviour

September 10, 2003

	Reports	Estimated cost to agencies Per day (000s)	Per year
Litter/rubbish	10,686	£1,866	£466m
Criminal damage/vandalism	7,855	£2,667	£667m
Vehicle-related nuisance	7,782	£1,361	£340m
Nuisance behaviour	7,660	£1,420	£355m
Intimidation/harassment	5,415	£1,983	£496m
Noise	5,374	£994	£249m
Rowdy behaviour	5,339	£665	£249m
Abandoned vehicles	4,994	£360	£90m
Street drinking and begging	3,239	£504	£126m
Drug misuse and dealing	2,920	£527	£132m
Animal-related problems	2,546	£458	£114m
Hoax calls	1,286	£198	£49m
Prostitution, kerb-crawling, sexual acts	1,011	£167	£42m
Total	**66,107**	**£13,500**	**£3,375bn**

Source: Telegraph Group Limited, London 2004

people who behaved badly. 'You can't be non-judgemental when you live next door to the family from hell,' Mr Blunkett added.

Ten cities have been selected for special action to tackle 'neighbours from hell', begging and graffiti. Birmingham, Manchester, Sheffield and Sunderland will focus on nuisance neighbours.

Brighton, Bristol, Leeds and the London boroughs of Camden and Westminster will clamp down on begging, while London and Liverpool will try to clear away abandoned cars.

Other areas, still to be identified, will be targeted for a '100 days cleanup' programme, attacking local priorities such as removing abandoned cars or graffiti.

There will be a hotline for people to inform on graffiti artists, backed by a national database to identify each paint vandal by their so-called 'tag' – the nickname or pseudonym they use.

Next year, a further 12 areas will pilot new powers to force the owners of telephone boxes, benches, bus shelters and other street furniture to clear up graffiti.

The move against beggars has been prompted by a survey showing that 65 per cent of people resented being approached and more than half felt threatened by people begging at cashpoints. The Home Office said three-quarters of beggars were heroin or crack cocaine addicts.

In an effort to ensure the courts treat anti-social behaviour seriously, a new team of specialists will start work in the Crown Prosecution Service to tackle the problem. It will issue guidance and devise training courses for prosecutors on how to handle low-level disorder offences.

The initiative will also try to clear away thousands of abandoned vehicles. Last year, some 300,000 cars were dumped. Another project will close off dark and dangerous alleyways often used as escape routes by criminals.

Ministers argue that neighbourhoods blighted by vandals feel and look unsafe, feed into people's fear of crime and encourage criminals and drug dealers to move in. However, the principal reason the yobs have taken over is because the police are less often seen on the streets.

Mr Blunkett said he wanted to find out why there are 36,000 more police today than 30 years ago yet fewer than ever are seen on patrol.

Reaction to the latest initiative ranged from the sceptical to the derisive. Norman Brennan, of the Victims of Crime Trust, said: 'The country could be forgiven for feeling that we've heard this all before.'

Oliver Letwin, the shadow home secretary, said: 'There are serious questions about whether it is just another headline-grabbing initiative, or whether it will bring lasting improvements.'

Jan Berry, the chairman of the Police Federation, said: 'It's extremely frustrating for police to try to remove some of these young people from the streets when they then see them going straight back on to the streets and no real sanctions are taking place.'

© Telegraph Group Limited, London 2004

How many victims?

Should we be scared or is it all over-hyped nonsense from the tabloids? TheSite puts it all in perspective

How many victims are there really?

- According to Home Office Recorded Crime Statistics there were 5.2 million offences recorded in the year ending March 2001, down 2.5% per cent on the previous 12 months.
- Violent crime accounted for 14% of all recorded crime yet over the past five years violent crime has fallen by 22%, domestic burglary is down by 39%, and vehicle crime is down by 26%.
- According to the *British Crime Survey*, in 2001/2002 3.5% of households were burgled, 7.1% of vehicle-owning households had items stolen from their vehicle, 1.7% a vehicle stolen, and 0.85 of adults were mugged.
- In 1997, there were over 1.6 million domestic burglaries in England and Wales. Burglary is the crime most commonly referred to Victim Support, with nearly half a million victims of burglary being offered help each year.
- It is estimated that one woman in four suffers domestic violence at some time in her life, and that domestic violence accounts for a quarter of all violent crime.
- According to the BCS (*British Crime Survey*) only 42% of all crime is reported to the police. The main reasons for not reporting included it being too trivial a matter; no real loss occurring or they considered it a private matter and dealt with it themselves.

So should I stay locked away in my house?

No, that would be far too drastic. Our fear of crime often exceeds the real risk: we live in a world where we are constantly bombarded by bad news and over-hyped headlines about soaring street crime levels, gun-toting kids running rife through the UK, and shootouts apparently happening on 'every' street corner.

The reality is a little different. Our fear has been pushed to new heights recently with more envisaged terrorist attacks following September 11. This is not a reason to panic or hide away from the big, bad world. This doesn't mean you should go to the other extreme and start leaving your doors unlocked and walking down dark alleys alone; just that a little perspective is needed here, people.

The statistics above show us that yes, crime happens, but often with a little common sense in keeping yourself and your possessions safe you can reduce your risk of becoming a victim.

- The above information is from YouthNet UK's web site TheSite.org which can be found at www.thesite.org

© thesite.org.uk

Crime against young people

Information from Victim Support

One in four young people aged 12 to 16 has been a victim of crime in the last year, according to research published by Victim Support in 2003. The research, carried out by NOP on over 400 young people across England and Wales, reveals some worrying trends. It suggests that the level of crime against this age group is consistent over time (similar numbers said the crime was up to three, six or twelve months ago), widespread and that it affects both boys and girls equally. Almost half (42%) of those who have been victims had been subjected to repeat incidents – with some reporting more than five incidents in the past year.

Of those who had been a victim of crime, the most common offences reported include violence and assault (54%), or theft (43%). Five per cent said that it was a sexual offence. Only 2% of victims specifically reported a mobile phone related crime, but many more who simply said that they had been a victim of theft or robbery could have been the victim of phone theft. The survey also focused on how young people were affected by being a victim and where they went to get help, support and information. Almost two-thirds (61%) said that they felt angry after the crime. Four out of ten (41%) said that they felt upset, a third (30%) shocked and one in five reported feeling frightened or worried (22% and 19%).

On a more positive note, the majority of the young people surveyed said that if they had been a victim, or were to become one, they would tell someone rather than suffering in silence – just 6% had told no one that a crime had happened. Of those who had already been a victim, 71% had told a parent or guardian, and 52% a friend. Four out of ten had told the police (40%) and around a third (29%) had told a teacher. But few had received specialist help from Victim Support or similar agencies, with just three out of the total sample group (less than 1%) having spoken to a professional support worker.

However, having heard more about Victim Support, an overwhelming 85% of all the young people surveyed said that they would find this kind of support helpful. Specifically they said that they would appreciate help in coping with their feelings after a crime (64%), advice or information (50%) or someone to speak to in confidence (49%). A quarter of the group (25%) said that they would like help dealing with schools, the police and other officials and a similar number (24%) wanted help in explaining the crime to parents. Yet according to the survey, six out of ten (60%) had never heard of Victim Support. This is in stark contrast to awareness of Victim Support among adults – according to the *British Crime Survey*, three-quarters of the adult population (74%) are aware of the charity.

Commenting on the findings, Dame Helen Reeves DBE, Chief Executive of Victim Support, said, 'It is clear that young people are more likely to suffer crime than adults and that their needs are being neglected. Even when they do go to the police it seems that they are not being referred for help. This can affect their attitudes to other people for the rest of their lives. It is vital that we act now to prevent any further neglect.' The charity plans to launch a number of pilot schemes for young victims around the country. Last year Victim Support's Witness Service helped almost 29,000 young people under 18 attending court as witnesses.

■ The above information is from Victim Support's web site which can be found at www.victimsupport.org

© *Victim Support*

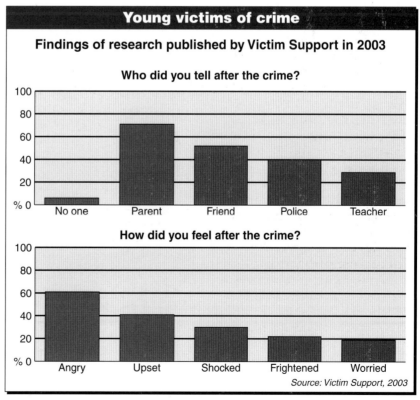

Young victims of crime

Findings of research published by Victim Support in 2003

Who did you tell after the crime?

How did you feel after the crime?

Source: Victim Support, 2003

Crime and social exclusion

Information from www.crimeinfo.org.uk

The basics

People find their way into crime and eventually prison for various reasons. For some it may seem to be their only option. For others it may be due to an irresistible opportunity, a rush of blood to the head or just simply to gain some kind of advantage, financial or otherwise. The truth is that there is no one single answer.

What we do know however is that many prisoners have poor education, housing problems, little job experience, and may have drink, drugs and mental health problems. If we want to understand how crime happens, why people end up in prison and how we can break the cycle of re-offending, we need to look at the range and extent of those problems.

Inside information

The social background of offenders
Compared with the general population, people in prison are:

- 13 times as likely to have been in care as a child.
- 13 times as likely to be unemployed.
- 10 times as likely to have been a regular truant.
- 2.5 times as likely to have had a family member convicted of a criminal offence.
- 6 times as likely to have been a young father.
- 15 times as likely to be HIV positive.

Basic skills

- 80 per cent of prisoners have writing skills at or below the level of an 11-year-old child.
- 65 per cent have numeracy skills at or below the level of an 11-year-old child.
- 50 per cent have reading skills at or below the level of an 11-year-old child.

Did you know?

These problems are even worse for 18- to 20-year-olds, whose basic skills, unemployment rate and school

the Centre for Crime and Justice Studies

exclusion background are all over a third worse than those of older prisoners.

Health background

- 60 to 70 per cent of prisoners were using drugs before imprisonment.
- Over 70 per cent suffer from at least two mental disorders.
- And 20 per cent of male and 37 per cent of female sentenced prisoners have attempted suicide in the past.
- Around half of prisoners had no GP before they came into custody.
- One prison drugs project found that although 70% of those entering the prison had a drug.

Many prisoners have poor education, housing problems, little job experience, and may have drink, drugs and mental health problems

---

misuse problem, 80% of these had never had any contact with drug treatment services.

The costs of prison
Imprisonment can make these problems worse. One in three prisoners will lose their house while in prison; two out of three will lose their job, and nearly half will lose contact with their family. Many prisoners find they develop drugs problems while inside. The result is that going to prison can make prisoners more likely to re-offend.

Re-offending
More than half of prisoners will commit another crime within 2 years of leaving prison. For men between the ages of 18 and 20 the rate is even higher. More than a third of prisoners will be back in prison on another sentence within two years. Research suggests that helping prisoners to tackle their education, mental health, drug and other problems can help them and give them a route out of crime.

Did you know?

Prisoners are over 20 times more likely than the general population to have been excluded from school.

■ The above information is from the web site www.crimeinfo.org.uk
© Centre for Crime and Justice Studies (CCJS)

Prison population

Key facts from the Prison Reform Trust

- On 30 January 2004 the prison population in England and Wales stood at 73,688, an increase of 2,779 over the past year.
- For the second consecutive year England and Wales has the highest imprisonment rate in the European Union at 141 per 100,000 of the population. Our imprisonment is significantly higher than our European neighbours. It is 44 per cent higher than Germany (98 per 100,000), and 52 per cent higher than France (93 per 100,000). It has risen dramatically over the last five years from 125 per 100,000 in 1999.
- The number of prisoners in England and Wales has increased by 25,000 in the last ten years. In 1994, the average prison population was 48,631. When Labour came to government in May 1997, the prison population was 60,131. Previously it took four decades (1954-1994) for the prison population to rise by 25,000.
- The number of women in prison has increased particularly dramatically. Ten years ago in 1994 the average female prison population was 1,811. Five years ago in 1999 it stood at 3,247. On 30 January 2004, there were 4,378 women in prison, an increase of 142 per cent in the last ten years.
- On 30 January 2004, there were 10,645 under- 21-year-olds in prisons in England and Wales. Of these, 2,489 were under 18.
- On 31 October 2003 there were 13,156 remand prisoners in England and Wales.
- Most of the rise in the prison population over the last decade can be explained by the significant increases in the proportion of offenders sent to prison and the length of sentences, particularly the increased number of long-term prisoners. On 31 May 2003, there were 26,299 serving sentences of four years and over. This compares with 14,750 in 1994, an increase of 80 per cent. In terms of custody rates, ten years ago one defendant in 26 would have gone into custody. Now it is one in 13. First-time domestic burglars are almost twice as likely to receive a custodial sentence today as they were eight years ago and at the same time the average sentence length for burglars has increased from 16 months to 18 months.
- The number of life sentence prisoners has increased considerably in recent years. There were 5,445 prisoners serving life sentences on 31 October 2003. This compares with fewer than 4,000 in 1998 and 3,000 in 1992. England and Wales has more life sentence prisoners than all of the member states of the European Union combined and has the highest number in the whole of Europe.
- The number of prisoners serving short sentences has also increased. Between 1992 and 2002 the number of adults sent to prison for sentences of less than 12 months more than doubled from 18,500 to nearly 48,000. In 2002 more than half of all those sent to prison were there for jail terms of six months or less.
- Over the last year prison overcrowding has been at its highest recorded level. At the end of December 2003, 81 of the 138 prisons in England and Wales were overcrowded.
- On 15 July 2003 over 16,000 prisoners were doubling up in cells designed for one (Parliamentary written answer 21 January 2003).
- Home Office projections over the next three years reveal that there is a huge gap between planned useable operational capacity and the forecast prison population.
- By the end of the decade Home Office projections predict a prison population of anything between 91,400 and 109,600.
- Since 1995, over 15,200 additional prison places have been provided at a cost of more than £2 billion (Hansard, written parliamentary answers September 2003).
- In an attempt to ease overcrowding, in April the Home Office ordered an emergency extension of the early release programme, the Home Detention Curfew (HDC). Prisoners can now leave custody under electronic surveillance up to four months before their release date. On 30 January 2004 there were 3,523 prisoners under HDC compared to 3,055 in January 2003.

Forecast prison population

	Planned average uncrowded capacity	Currently planned average useage operational capacity	Forecast average population
2007	70,400	78,700	88,700
2006	69,500	78,750	87,200
2005	69,000	78,200	81,500
2004	67,000	75,800	76,200

Source: Prison Reform Trust

- Research by the Prime Minister's Strategy Unit highlighted in the Carter report (*Managing Offenders, Reducing Crime*, December 2003) says that a 22 per cent increase in the prison population since 1997 is estimated to have reduced crime by around five per cent during a period when overall crime fell by 30 per cent. The report states: 'There is no convincing evidence that further increases in the use of custody would significantly reduce crime'.
- Prison has a poor record in reducing re-offending – 59 per cent of prisoners are reconvicted within two years of being released. The reconviction rate for male young adults (under 21) over the same period is 74 per cent. For prisoners who are sentenced for

Sentenced population by offence type

Offence group	Male	Female	Total
Violence against the person	12,387	535	12,922
Sexual offences	5,463	0	5,463
Burglary	8,486	243	8,729
Robbery	7,733	397	8,130
Theft and handling	4,230	493	4,723
Fraud and forgery	905	104	1,009
Drug offences	8,850	1,318	10,168
Motoring offences	2,601	50	2,651
Other	3,928	226	4,154
Not recorded	839	35	874
Total	**55,422**	**3,401**	**58,823**

Source: Prison Reform Trust, May 2003

burglary, one of the most common offences, the reconviction rate is 76 per cent.

- The Social Exclusion Unit has concluded that re-offending by ex-prisoners costs society at least £11 billion per year. Ex-prisoners are responsible for about one in five of all recorded crimes.

■ The above information is from the Prison Reform Trust's web site: www.prisonreformtrust.org.uk

© *Prison Reform Trust*

What's prison really like?

Information from HMP & YOI PARC

'*Coming to prison ruins your life. I regret what I did so much. It's only when you're in prison and you have time to think that you realise what you've thrown away by coming here.*'
22-year-old young offender serving six months for possession with intent to supply drugs

'*The worst thing about being in prison is that you miss your family and all the important events in their lives. My daughter was born while I was in here. She'll be over a year old when I get out.*'
30-year-old prisoner serving two years four months for aggravated burglary

'*You get a really bad feeling when you come through the main gates of the prison, as you know that it will be some time before you get your freedom back.*'
19-year-old young offender serving 12 months for possession with intent to supply

'*Since I have been in prison I have lost everything – my girlfriend, belongings, family, friends and freedom. I am expecting a long sentence in prison for a*

crime that wasn't worth anything in the world.'
26-year-old prisoner on remand for charges of aggravated burglary and possession of cocaine

Life behind bars: a prisoner's typical day
6am: Morning Roll Count

7am: Servery workers woken up to prepare breakfast for other prisoners

7.30am: Remaining prisoners woken up for breakfast – typically toast/cereal

8am: Prisoners locked up in cells

8.40am: Prisoners who attend Education classes unlocked – they return to the wing at 11.40am

11am: Remaining prisoners unlocked for association – talking to other prisoners, playing pool etc.

12 noon: Lunch – typically curry and chips, sliced bread, jam sponge and custard

12.40pm: Prisoners locked up in cells for Roll Count

1.40pm: Prisoners who attend Education unlocked – they return to their wings at 4.45pm

4.15pm: Prisoners who do not work or attend Education unlocked for exercise

4.45pm: Exercise for those attending Education or work on wing yard

5.15pm: Prisoners locked up

5.30pm: Evening Roll Count

6.15pm: Unlocked for tea and association – chess, draughts, pool etc. Time here for phone calls to family and friends

8pm: Prisoners on standard regime locked up in cells – Roll Count

9pm: Prisoners on enhanced regime locked up in cells – Final Roll Count

© *HMP PARC*

Through the eyes of children

Youth crime is a huge problem for which there are no simple solutions. The Magistrate wanted to give the chance to children to have their say. Children's Express, spoke to children and teenagers from across London, all of whom had a different story to tell.

Alfred, 10: a victim of bullying, North London

It should be every child's right to feel safe in the area they live in. But Alfred, 10, from Islington, is not so lucky.

He's unable to lead a normal life because for years he's been the victim of bullying on the council estate where he lives: 'I'm too scared to walk around my estate on my own because there's a group of older kids who bully me.'

He doesn't even feel safe walking to school on his own, even though it's only a few minutes down the road: 'I'm scared that they'll be hiding around the corner waiting for me,' he says.

Alfred has good reason to be afraid. He's been kicked and punched so many times he's lost count. On one occasion he was so badly beaten, he had to go to hospital in an ambulance.

As if that wasn't bad enough, the boy who beat up Alfred still lives in the same block of flats so his parents will not let him even step foot outside his front door: 'They're worried about me in case I get hurt again.'

It's understandable that Alfred feels angry. He says it's not fair that he has to stay inside all the time just because of a bunch of 'stupid kids'.

Alfred reckons it's quite possible that kids like him who get picked on will turn into bullies themselves because it's one way of dealing with the problem: 'I do worry that one day I might end up doing the same kinds of things. If you hang out with bullies, at least you won't get beaten up,' he says.

'When I was in a gang, I was with all my brethren . . . when you're in a gang, no one messes with you'

But Alfred adds that he also knows that if he did start hanging out with the wrong crowd, he'd probably 'get chucked in jail'. So even though it is frustrating that he can't go out without his big sister always being there, he'd rather stay inside if it means he stays away from the kids on his estate.

We asked Alfred why he thought the young people on his estate liked bullying younger kids. He said it was because there was nothing else to do: 'You're not allowed to play ball games and you can't use the football pitch any more. It's boring for a lot of kids, so they go around beating up other kids.

'I don't think the council does enough for us. They could at least fix up our park,' he adds.

Sam, 17, and John, 16: caught up in gang culture, East London

It's true that gang culture is sometimes glorified in violent films and rap lyrics but is it really the only reason young people are attracted to gangs?

Sam, 17, from Hackney is no longer in a gang but in his early teens he spent three years in one. He found it difficult to explain to us why he first got involved: 'You get a little party happening. You might just hang out and . . . I don't really know . . .'

But what Sam does know, is that being in a gang made him feel as though he was a part of something in which he belonged. He liked the closeness and the solidarity: 'Gangs are like friends, deep friends, you know what I mean? They're like proper friends. When I was in a gang, I was with all my brethren.'

As strange as it may sound, for Sam it was also about safety because as he said: 'When you're in a gang, no one messes with you.'

Jack, 15: picked out for being black, North London

A lot of people believe that the answer to reducing youth crime lies in more policing but for many young people putting more officers on the beat isn't enough. What's just as important, if not more so, is that young people are able to relate to police, especially if they're children and teenagers from ethnic minorities.

Jack, 15, from Holloway has very little faith in the police and for good reason – he's been stopped more times than he can remember and he's never committed a crime in his life. It'll come as no surprise to learn that Jack is black.

'The first time it happened I was only 12 years old. I've been stopped load of times since then. I don't know why it happens to me, I just know it happens ... it's probably because I'm black.'

Jack reckons young black men are an easy target for the police because they hang around in large groups. But he says this doesn't mean they have the right to assume he's doing something wrong just because he's hanging out with his mates:

'I don't carry a knife on me. I'm not doing anything silly, so there's no way they could arrest me for anything. I just don't see why they're bothering me, It's out of order.'

Since the Stephen Lawrence inquiry the general public have been led to believe that racism in the police force is being addressed. But Jack is sceptical: 'I don't think anything's changed. There's still a lot of racism around, it's just less obvious.'

John, 16, is also from Hackney and like Sam he also got involved with his gang when he was in his early teens. He's still very much involved with the gang so understandably he was reluctant to tell us too much about what they got up to.

He didn't have any answers as to why he'd joined but to us John appeared proud of the lifestyle he led and we noticed that he kept his probation tag on show throughout the interview, as if to remind us he'd been in trouble with the law.

We asked John and Sam if the stories of gang members carrying weapons in the media were just wild exaggerations. Both replied that it was normal to carry them. In fact Sam said he'd carried a knife when he was in a gang but added that if he had still been involved, he'd be carrying a gun by now, because it was the new weapon of choice.

John agreed, adding that if he wanted a gun, he'd have no problems whatsoever in getting a hold of one: 'I know people who could easily get me a gun.'

Although Sam has now left the gang, he says he wasn't able to leave on his own accord. It was only when he got put in a young offenders' institute, that he broke ties with them.

John's never been 'put away' but he reckons it's only because he's wearing a tag around his ankle: 'I'm wearing this so I've got to stay out of trouble.' What's even sadder, is that for John it wasn't a case of 'if' he gets put in prison but 'when':

'I'll stop when I go to Feltham.'

'Police officers don't have respect for teenagers on the street. If anything happened to me, I wouldn't go to the police because I know they'd treat me more like the criminal than the victim.

'I'd like the police to just take teenagers on the whole a lot more seriously,' he adds.

Sam, 13: staying away from drugs, East London

Can you imagine being so afraid of the school toilets, you'd prefer to hold on all day long?

As horrible as it sounds, it's a reality for a lot of young people in London secondary schools. Why? Because it's a well-known fact at some schools that you only go to the toilet if you want to take drugs.

'I never go to the toilets because I'm too scared,' says Sam, 13 from East London.

'There's gangs everywhere and you know that at my school if you're going to the toilet you're most certainly going there to do drugs.'

Sam's now in Year 9 which means he can leave the school grounds at lunch, so he just waits until then to use the toilet. But when he was in Year 7 and 8 he reckons he'd just hold on for the whole day.

The one time Sam did brave the school toilets he came face to face with a boy in Year 11 who was taking drugs: 'He had tin foil and white powder, which looked kind of like chalk. He was smoking it. I looked at him and told him not to worry, that I wouldn't grass. Then he said "Do you want some?"'

Sam was so frightened that the boy would 'batter him' he reckons that for a split second he considered accepting his offer but instead just tried to act as though it wasn't a big deal:

'I just told him next time and then walked out.'

■ The names in this article have been changed to protect the young people who were interviewed.

About the team

This story was produced by James Jordan, 10, Nestor Sayo, 11, Samir Pasha, 13, Tracey Jordan, 14, Ashleigh Jordan, 12, Horia El Hadad, 16, Fola Egbewole, 16. It was published in *The Magistrate*.

■ The above information is from Children's Express's web site which can be found at www.childrens-express.org

© *Children's Express*

One in four teenagers commits a crime

More than one in four of all teenagers – about 1.25 million of all young people – have committed a criminal offence in the last 12 months, according to a draft official report on youth justice seen by the *Guardian*.

Juvenile crime is now estimated by the Audit Commission to cost the economy more than £10bn a year and accounts for nearly a fifth of the total annual cost of crime.

The yet-to-be published report into the youth justice system says the number of known juvenile offenders has actually fallen since a peak in 1992 alongside the drop in overall recorded crime.

But it warns that the number of juveniles cautioned or convicted for violence, drug offences and robbery has risen and the number locked away in secure facilities increased steadily during the 1990s before beginning to level off.

A draft copy of a separate report on youth justice from the National Audit Office (NAO), Whitehall's spending watchdog, also seen by the *Guardian*, warns that some youth jails are failing to provide education and other programmes for those in their care.

The unpublished NAO report goes on to say that children who are getting some kind of education while they are locked away are only able to continue it when they leave custody in very few areas. The official report identifies this as one of the main reasons why 84% of young offenders released from detention reoffend within two years.

The NAO report says the latest unpublished juvenile crime figures show that 268,500 young people aged 10 to 17 in England and Wales were arrested in 2002/03 – about 5% of their age group. This is more than twice the 2.4% arrest rate for the adult population.

The courts in England and Wales last year sentenced 93,200

By Alan Travis, Home Affairs Editor

young offenders, of whom 64% received a community sentence, 7% were sent to custody and the remainder were fined or discharged.

The Audit Commission inquiry was designed as a follow-up to its 1996 report, *Misspent Youth*, which found that the existing system for dealing with youth crime was inefficient and expensive, and that services were failing both young offenders and their victims.

268,500 young people aged 10 to 17 in England and Wales were arrested in 2002/03 – about 5% of their age group

In response, the government set up the youth justice board in 1998 and a network of youth offending teams to work with juvenile offenders across England and Wales. Ministers also promised to halve the time taken by the courts to deal with young offenders from 142 days to 71 days or fewer. This pledge was met in July 2001.

A draft preface to the Audit Commission's report says its research

found that five years later 'the new arrangements are a significant improvement and a good model for delivering public services' with the youth offending teams critical to their effectiveness.

But it also concludes that resources need to be redistributed to focus more on serious and persistent young offenders and that the confidence of the courts and the public in alternatives to custody needs to be improved.

The draft Audit Commission report also concludes that schools need to play a more central role in preventing youth offending.

The NAO report reaches similar conclusions and highlights recent research which suggests 60% of children excluded from school committed an offence last year, compared with 26% of children at school.

It also concludes that the youth justice board (YJB) has made good progress and is beginning to have an impact on reoffending rates.

But it says it will have to improve the credibility of higher tariff community sentences for juveniles, which have a reoffending rate of around 60%, if it is to persuade the courts to reduce the number of young people placed in custody.

'Even a small shift in numbers could release significant resources for prevention work and improving the quality of both community sentences and custodial programmes provided,' says the draft NAO report.

It says that the courts have welcomed the introduction of a new higher tariff community sentence – the intensive supervision and surveillance programme – but some areas have reported high breach rates with some young offenders being re-sentenced to custody. It also warns it is being used instead of existing community penalties rather than as an alternative to prison.

Young people and crime

Youth Justice Board Youth Survey 2003

Overall levels of offending among young people have remained constant since 2002. Nonetheless, there has been an increase in the average number of crimes committed by young offenders, a drop in detection rates and a marginal increase in the proportion of young people who re-offend. The findings do suggest, however, that young offenders are now far more likely to receive some form of punishment as a consequence of being caught.

The most common crime which young people are a victim of is being threatened by others, typically by someone under the age of 18. The people they turn to, as a result of being a victim of crime, are their parents or their friends. However, excluded young people are more likely to report the incident to the police or to deal with the situation themselves. Indeed, excluded young people typically express lower levels of concern for their personal safety, but the findings suggest that they are more likely to be exposed to crime and become a victim of crime than mainstream school pupils.

While young people in mainstream schools feel that most criminal activities are wrong to do, no matter what the situation is, the proportion saying that each activity is wrong is declining year-on-year. In contrast, although excluded young people are less likely to recognise the majority activities as being wrong their sense of right and wrong does not appear to be declining. Truancy rates among mainstream pupils has dropped, but remain constant among excluded young people, who are more likely to play truant. Playing truant typically starts in Year 7 or below. Moreover, the age at which young people start playing truant reflects the age at which young people start offending. Although there is no clear indication as to which comes first, truancy or offending, the findings suggest a strong correlation between the two.

Setting the findings in context

MORI conducted two separate studies of young people; a survey of 4,963 11 to 16-year-olds in mainstream education and a survey of 586 young people excluded from school, currently attending a special project.

The profile of the two samples of young people, those in mainstream education and those who have been excluded, does vary and this needs to be taken into account when considering the findings. In comparison to mainstream pupils, excluded young people are more likely to be male and in the older age groups. This profile mirrors that of offenders.

The most common crime which young people are a victim of is being threatened by others, typically by someone under the age of 18

The household profile of excluded young people also differs. They are more likely to live in single-parent households than young people in mainstream schools and have a parent/step-parent that is neither in part-time or full-time employment.

Levels of offending and the crimes committed

Levels of offending remain consistent, and as with previous years, excluded pupils are far more likely to offend than young people in mainstream schools.

- 26% of mainstream young people say they have committed an offence in the last 12 months.
- 60% of excluded young people say they have committed an offence in the last 12 months.

The offences most likely to be committed by offenders in mainstream schools and offenders who have been excluded from school differ slightly.

- The most common offences committed by mainstream offenders are:
  – travelling on a bus, train or underground without paying the fare (53%);
  – hurting someone but not leading to them needing medical attention (41%).

The most common offences committed by excluded offenders are:

- hurting someone but not leading to them needing medical attention (62%);
- carrying a knife (62%).

While the overall proportion of young people who commit offences has not increased since 2002, the findings indicate that offenders (excluded or mainstream pupils) are committing more offences. For example the average number of offences has risen from four per mainstream offender in 2002 to five each in 2003, and from 10 in 2002 to 11 per excluded offender in 2003. Among young offenders in mainstream schools, the biggest increases are apparent in the two most common crimes: Travelling on a bus, train or underground without paying the fare has increased from 46% in 2002 to 53% in 2003. There is a similar increase in the proportion reporting to have hurt someone but they did not need medical attention (up from 33% in 2002 to 41% in 2003).

Offences committed by excluded pupils which show the biggest increase year-on-year are: Beating up someone not in their family (49% in 2003 vs. 38% in 2002). Threatening or assaulting others in public (57% in 2003 vs. 48% in 2002). Stealing anything from their home (21% in 2003 vs. 13% in 2002).

Violent crime in general rose in 2003 among both mainstream and excluded young offenders. These offences, such as assaulting or threatening others, continue to be far more prevalent among excluded young offenders than among young people in school.

The profile of offenders

The profile of offenders is similar to previous years. Offenders tend to be:
- Male

A third (32%) of boys in mainstream education have committed an offence, compared with 20% of girls. While the difference is not so marked among excluded pupils the pattern is still notable: Three in five excluded boys (61%) have offended, compared with 56% of girls.

- Older pupils

Only 14% of 11-year-olds in mainstream education have offended compared with 39% of 15- to 16-year-olds. Among excluded pupils, 43% of 11-year-olds have offended compared with 61% of 15- to 16 year olds. The fact that there is a higher level of offending at a younger age among excluded pupils than their peers in mainstream education, ties in with the fact that excluded young people are more likely to start committing offences at a younger age.

One in eight mainstream and excluded offenders committed their first offence when they were seven years of age or younger (12% and 13%, respectively). That said, the key watershed ages for starting to offend are between 11 and 13, with 38% of mainstream and 41% of excluded offenders reporting this as the age they first committed an offence.

In line with 2002, the research finds that young people who offend typically do so with their friends, rather than alone or with siblings. This finding is common to both mainstream and excluded offenders:
- 61% of offenders in mainstream education and 67% of excluded offenders usually commit offences *with friends*.
- 22% of offenders in mainstream education and 24% of excluded offenders are usually *on their own* when they commit offences.

Girls are more likely to commit crimes with their friends. This ties in

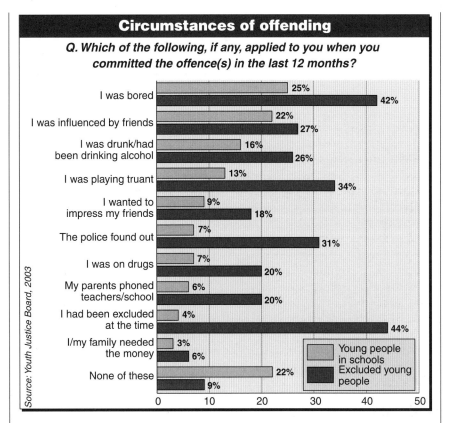

Circumstances of offending

Q. Which of the following, if any, applied to you when you committed the offence(s) in the last 12 months?

Source: Youth Justice Board, 2003

	Young people in schools	Excluded young people
I was bored	25%	42%
I was influenced by friends	22%	27%
I was drunk/had been drinking alcohol	16%	26%
I was playing truant	13%	34%
I wanted to impress my friends	9%	18%
The police found out	7%	31%
I was on drugs	7%	20%
My parents phoned teachers/school	6%	20%
I had been excluded at the time	4%	44%
I/my family needed the money	3%	6%
None of these	22%	9%

with the types of offences they carry out, such as shoplifting or writing or spraying graffiti.

Boredom, peer pressure and being drunk are the reasons typically cited for offending behaviour (this is consistent with the findings from previous surveys).
- 25% of offenders in mainstream education and 42% of excluded offenders said they were bored.
- 22% of offenders in mainstream education and 27% of excluded offenders say they were influenced by friends.
- 16% of mainstream and 26% of excluded offenders were drunk at the time of the last offence they committed.
- 13% of mainstream and 34% of excluded offenders were playing truant when they last offended.

Excluded young offenders are more likely to have been playing truant or been found out by the police at the time of committing their last offence, than their peers in mainstream schools. This may relate to the fact that far higher proportions of excluded young people, in comparison with their mainstream peers, play truant.

Outcomes of offending

There has been a drop in the proportion of young offenders who are caught by the police since 2001.[1]
- 21% of offenders in mainstream education and 69% of excluded offenders were caught by the police in 2003, compared with 28% and 71% in 2001.

Excluded offenders are more likely to be caught by the police than offenders in mainstream education, which is consistent with the findings from previous studies. Moreover, the consequences of being caught continue to be harsher for excluded young offenders, specifically in terms of having to attend court and being referred to a Youth Offending Team.

While there may have been a drop in the proportion of young offenders caught by the police, the likelihood of receiving some form of punishment as a consequence of being caught has increased over the last two years:
- In 2001 22% of mainstream pupils who self-reported committing an offence said nothing happened to them as a result of being caught, compared with just 9% who say nothing happened in 2003.
- Similarly, in 2003 only 3% of excluded offenders said nothing happened as a consequence of being caught, compared with 12% in 2001.

Young people who are caught offending typically receive a final warning as a result (55% of excluded pupils, 42% of those in mainstream schools). This is consistent with the 2001 Youth Survey. However, the findings indicate an increase in the use of other types of punishments, in particular:

- More young offenders are having to apologise to victims since 2001. Over a quarter (27%) of offenders who are mainstream pupils were made to apologise to the victim in 2003, compared with 20% of offenders in 2001. Among excluded offenders the proportion having to apologise to the victim increased from 24% to 36%.
- More offenders in mainstream schools are having to pay fines, an increase of 17% compared to 11% in 2001.
- Twice as many mainstream offenders are also now having to go to court, an increase from 7% in 2001 to 14% in 2003.
- Nearly three times as many excluded offenders are having to do work in the community (17% in 2003 compared to 6% in 2001).

A significant proportion of young offenders – in both mainstream and excluded education – say that they are not as likely to re-offend having been caught by the police. However, in reality well over half have re-offended.

- 44% of mainstream offenders and 39% from excluded projects say being caught has impacted on their likelihood of re-offending.
- 57% of those in mainstream schools and 75% of those in excluded projects who have been caught offending say they have re-offended.

Indeed, there has been a marginal increase in the proportion of young people – both those in mainstream education and those who are excluded – who re-offend after being caught by the police. In addition, even though they are more likely to be caught and the consequences are often harsher, a higher proportion of excluded young people re-offend, than offenders in mainstream education.

Linked to this is the fact that excluded young people are far less likely to say that the fear of being caught deters them from committing crime, than young people in mainstream education (34% and 47%, respectively). The reactions of their parents is most likely to deter excluded young people (38%).

Note
1   The 2002 data are not comparable.

- Reproduced by kind permission of the Youth Justice Board for England and Wales. The above is an extract from the summary of the Youth Justice Board's *Youth Survey 2003*. See page 41 for their address details.

© Reproduced by kind permission of the Youth Justice Board for England and Wales

Under-16s experience of and attitudes to crime

Crimestoppers survey

Introduction

- The first major piece of research into under-16s' (i.e. non-adult) experience of and attitudes to crime, revealing for the first time the hidden truth about the extent of crime in the UK.
- The survey aims to complete the picture of crime in the UK (the *British Crime Survey* only interviews adults over 16 years despite the widely accepted view that a significant proportion of crime is committed by and against under-16s).
- A representative nationwide survey of 1,064 male and female youths, aged 10-15 years old, who

have been interviewed on their experiences of and attitudes towards crime.

Results

Fear of crime
- 42% of 10- to 15-year-olds in the UK are very worried about crime (amongst boys the figure is 35% rising to 48% amongst girls).

Fear based on personal experience of crime, or the experience of friends/siblings
- 18% of under-15s have been a victim of crime (22% male vs. 15% female).
- 23% of these crime victims were mugged or the victims of street crime.
- 7% of victims had been a victim of crime on two or more occasions.
- A staggering 16 respondents (2%) had been the victim of crime on more than five separate occasions
- 31% had a friend, brother or sister who had been a victim of crime.
- 12% (1 in 8) of all respondents had a friend, brother or sister who

had been a victim of crime twice or more.

- One in four (25%) had a friend, brother or sister who had had a mobile phone or bicycle stolen.

40% of victims under 16 know the identity of their assailant

- In an amazing 40% of cases, the person committing the crime was known to the victim either by sight or by name.
- In 23% of cases, where the respondent had been a victim of crime more than once, the perpetrator was the same person.

Young reluctant to tell parents/police when they've been a victim of crime

- Almost half of children (45%) did not tell their parents.
- Over half (51%) did not tell the police.

Anonymity

The appeal of being able to give information on crime anonymously (Crimestoppers).

- Almost 4 out of 10 (38%) of all respondents said they would be more likely to give information on crime if there was a method of doing so without giving their name.

The key element of Crimestoppers' phonelines (0800 555 111) is that they guarantee anonymity to the caller. This means that many of the reasons given by victims under 16 for not giving information no longer apply. For example:

- 40% said it was not worth reporting or that nothing could be done about it.
- 10% dislike getting involved with the police.
- 16% were afraid of getting beaten up or did not want to inform on someone he or she knew.

Other interesting information to come out of the survey

Under-16s' biggest worries about crime

- One in four (26%) were most worried about theft, including mugging (13%) and burglary (10%).
- One in eight (13%) were most worried about drugs.
- 5% were most worried about crimes involving weapons (four respondents cited their greatest worry as being shot).
- A further 3% (28 respondents) responded that their biggest worry about crime in their area is murder.

What would young people do to cut down crime?

- 61% say more police are needed on the street.
- 41% say kids should be given more to do outside school.
- 29% say something should be done about drugs.
- 26% want longer jail sentences.
- 22% want more protection at school.
- 20% want a crackdown on young criminals.
- 17% want someone to talk to about crime either at school or on a helpline.

Drugs – perhaps surprisingly, those surveyed seemed to take a consistently stern view of drugs, suggesting that society's anti-drugs messages may be starting to get through:

- Asked to rate taking drugs out of ten on a scale of seriousness, respondents gave a mean figure of 8.79.
- 43% of respondents said they were afraid of people on drugs, with only teenage gangs at 46% figuring higher on interviewees' list of fears.
- When asked what they most blame for crime today, 'people selling or taking drugs' came top with 55% of all respondents' votes.

Decline in fear of traditional figures of authority? When asked who they were frightened of, under-16s answered as follows:

- 45% Teenage gangs
- 43% People on drugs
- 40% Drunks
- 26% Bullies at school
- 23% Not frightened of anybody
- 21% People asking for money
- 16% Racists
- 15% Older kids
- 8% The police
- 6% Kids your own age
- 5% Head teacher
- 3% Father
- 2% Mother.

What do under-16s most blame for crime today?

- 55% People selling/taking drugs
- 43% Children/teenagers breaking the law
- 38% Parents not controlling or disciplining children
- 32% Police not interested
- 30% Nothing to do outside school hours
- 24% Things shown on TV
- 20% Films
- 18% Schools not giving the right discipline
- 7% Music videos.

- The survey was conducted by Carrick James on behalf of Crimestoppers Trust. 1,064 people between the ages of 10 and 15, covering the social spectrum, were questioned across the UK.

© Crimestoppers

Focus on crime

Young people are often seen as a cause of the nation's rising crime rate.

But what do young people themselves think about the rise in crime? Are they concerned, ambivalent or accepting?

The Norwich Union *Youth Insight Report* captures their thoughts, fears and experiences of crime.

Have they been a victim of crime themselves, or do they know someone who has? And what's the impact on their own community – are they worried for their personal safety and that of their family?

Norwich Union has spoken to over 600 young people between the ages of 13 and 19 across the country from differing social backgrounds. And there is a feeling amongst teens that crime DOES in fact pay.

More than half think that crime pays – despite four in five worrying about becoming a victim of crime themselves.

For many, the benefits of crime outweigh the possible consequences – even if it means time behind bars.

But who do young people listen to and who do they think is responsible for helping make the streets safer for all generations?

Not surprisingly, young people would like to see the police doing more to reduce crime.

But they also put their hands up and admit that they too have a role to play in reducing crime.

It is startling that nearly a third of socially excluded young people accept that crime is part of their society. And over 80 per cent of those interviewed knew someone who had been involved in crime.

It's statistics like these that have led Norwich Union to join forces with the national crime reduction organisation, Crime Concern.

The partnership has been responsible for launching the Norwich Union Neighbourhood Apprenticeship Scheme, which tackles crime at grassroots level.

The scheme empowers individuals to tackle crime in the areas that need it most by training local people to become neighbourhood apprentices within their own communities.

Three apprentices have recently been appointed on housing estates in Chester, Birmingham and London.

They are working with experienced Crime Concern managers to implement crime reduction programmes. A key part of the apprentice's brief is to work with young people to combat some of the frustrations and pressures that can lead to crime.

The majority of young people are not blasé about crime. Over half [55 per cent] are worried about themselves or their family being victims of crime

---

This report is not about attributing blame but understanding young people's attitudes to crime and looking for solutions to help reduce it.

Key findings

Experience of crime

Eighty-five per cent of young people think crime is getting worse. This is not surprising when you learn that two-thirds of young people have either been victims of crime or know someone who has.

In socially deprived areas, crime is part of the fabric of many young people's lives – 94 per cent of teens have experienced crime. Four in five admit they know someone who has committed a crime.

Young people's experience of crime is varied. Most commonly, teens are victims of assault or street theft [30 per cent]. However, in the London Borough of Hackney, one in three teens revealed they had experience of gun crime.

Mobile phone theft is far more common in the South-East. In London, 40 per cent of teens have been victims of mobile phone theft. This figure rises to 60 per cent in socially deprived areas of the capital.

Fear of crime

The majority of young people are not blasé about crime. Over half [55 per cent] are worried about themselves or their family being victims of crime. A third accepted that crime was part of their society.

Regionally teenagers from London were the most concerned about crime – just four per cent admitted they were not worried. However, 15 per cent of young people from Birmingham were not worried about crime.

The most serious offences were considered to be gun crime, followed by drug dealing and assault. Vandalism, shoplifting and mobile phone theft were seen as the least severe.

Does crime pay?

The phrase 'crime doesn't pay' no longer rings true for UK teens.

On a national level over 40 per cent of young people feel that crime does pay and within socially deprived areas this figure rises to almost 60 per cent.

For many teenagers the material benefits of crime outweigh the risks of punishment or even the punishment itself.

Respect

Despite the nation's obsession with sporting and music stars, young people respect their parents and see family members as strong role models.

When asked who they most respected, the majority of young people [64 per cent] named their parents. Interestingly nearly half [49 per cent] of teens from socially deprived areas named their mother as the person they most respect. Just two per cent named their father.

When the question was reversed to determine who young people least respected, nearly half [44 per cent] stated the Government. Within socially deprived areas almost a third [32 per cent] of teens named the police.

As well as not respecting the Government, 84 per cent of young people think the Government and its views are too far removed from their day-to-day lives.

Norwich Union also asked young people about their role models. Surprisingly nearly half [49 per cent] did not have any role models. Of those who did, the majority [24 per cent] named family members over celebrities, friends or sports people. Other role models varied greatly from David Beckham, Britney Spears, Ms Dynamite and 50 Cent to God, Jamie Oliver, Stephen Hawking and Martin Luther King.

Sense of community
Out of touch at 40?
Well, if you're 40 years or older you are out of touch according to young people in Britain. Nearly four in five believe that older people are out of touch with teenagers.

When asked at what age people lose touch with teenagers, the majority agreed that 40 is the cut-off point between young and old.

Despite the gap between the generations, 70 per cent of young people feel part of a community. This figure rises to 78 per cent within socially deprived areas.

Youth Insight Report – solutions
The role of apprentices
Norwich Union has partnered Crime Concern to develop and fund a pilot apprenticeship scheme – the Norwich Union Neighbourhood Apprenticeship Scheme.

This scheme focuses on training and coaching local people to become accredited neighbourhood community apprentices within their own communities.

The apprentices work under the supervision and guidance of experienced Crime Concern managers already working on three-year crime reduction programmes in deprived neighbourhoods across the country.

Norwich Union Neighbourhood Apprentices have been appointed at three estates across the country:

Northfield Estate, Birmingham. Northfield is made up of five estates with a population of more than 10,000. Young people and anti-social behaviour has been identified as one of the major issues affecting the area. A recent fear of crime survey showed that 70 per cent of residents reported lack of facilities for young people as a cause of anti-social behaviour and almost two-thirds reported young people hanging around in groups on the estate as a problem and increased fear of crime.

Blacon Estate, Chester. Blacon has a population of 14,500 residents. Young people and anti-social behaviour are seen as a major problem affecting residents and our Norwich Union apprentice will work with the Blacon team to address this issue.

Stamford Hill, Hackney, London. Stamford Hill is a largely multi-cultural area with a key focus on youth inclusion. As part of the apprenticeship scheme, the Norwich Union apprentice has been working closely with the youth inclusion programme on the estate.

About Norwich Union
Norwich Union is the largest general insurer in the UK, insuring one in five vehicles on the road, one in five households and over 700,000 businesses across the UK.

Norwich Union products are available through a variety of distribution channels including brokers, corporate partners such as banks and building societies and Norwich Union Direct. www.norwich-union.co.uk

About the report
Norwich Union Insurance commissioned Brands & Issues to interview 510 young people throughout the UK aged between 13 and 19 in July 2003. A further 138 interviews were conducted with young people living in socially deprived areas in Chester, Hackney and Birmingham during August 2003.

Within the *Youth Insight Report* the term crime relates to the following: gun crime, burglary, assault, theft, mugging, joy riding, vandalism, graffiti, shoplifting, fraud, speeding and drug dealing.

© *Norwich Union*

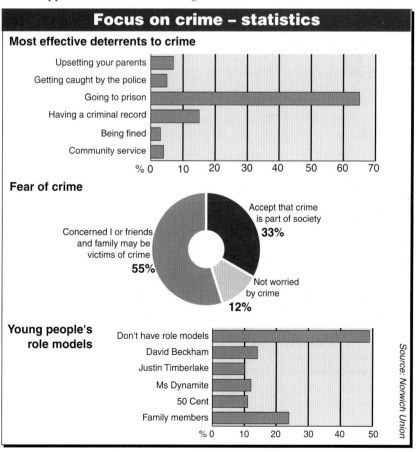

Focus on crime – statistics

Most effective deterrents to crime

Fear of crime

Young people's role models

Source: Norwich Union

Better than cure?

Youth Inclusion Programmes are targeted at crime prevention, as Clare Harvey explains

When 15-year-old Mandy was referred to her local Youth Inclusion Programme (YIP) in 2003, teachers had almost given up hope. She was a frequent truant and when at school she was sullen and disruptive. Now, just a few months on, Mandy starts her final school year with one GCSE equivalent already under her belt. She's also joined a young women's group, 'Soul Sisters', and 'SE1', a music-based community club.

'Mandy is a good example of the young people we work with,' says Richard Leahy, Education co-ordinator with the Kickstart YIP in south-east London. 'What she needed, and what the school was unable to give her, was some individual attention. She's been coming to our tutorials and went away on a couple of residential weekends and she's a different girl now. It's great to see.'

Prevention strategy

In the past, Mandy might have 'fallen through the net', with increasing truancy leading to a lack of formal qualifications and potential involvement with crime. However, Youth Justice Board introduced YIPs in the late 1990s to tackle the problems facing young people like Mandy.

YIPs started at around the same time as Youth Offending Teams (YOTs), with a similar multi-agency approach: police, social workers, probation officers and teachers work together to help specific youngsters. The difference is that whilst YOTs work with young people who have already entered the Criminal Justice System, the idea of YIPs is preventative: by working with young people showing signs of difficulty at an earlier stage, the aim is to halt the downward spiral from truancy and antisocial behaviour to crime.

The idea of YIPs is preventative: by working with young people showing signs of difficulty at an earlier stage

---

There are currently 70 YIPs, set up in the most deprived areas of England and Wales. Around two-thirds are managed by Youth Offending Teams; the remainder are run by the charity Crime Concern. Each targets 50 specific 13- to 16-year-olds deemed by a panel of social workers, police, teachers and youth

workers to be most 'at risk' of social exclusion. In order to engage with the 50 in question, however, YIPs are fairly broad, running projects aimed at all young people in a given area. Activities range from community clubs and cafés through to DJ workshops, sports, residentials, as well as more structured work, such as the tutorials on offer at the Kickstart YIP.

Multi-agency working

Four years on from their inception, and with government funding promised until 2006, how well are YIPs working?

So far, the results appear impressive, with studies showing a 30% reduction in reported neighbourhood crime, a 60% reduction in youth arrest rates and a 30% reduction in school exclusion (Crime Concern figures, 2003), but that's not the full picture, says Crime Concern's Jo Burden: 'Those kinds of statistics don't demonstrate the fantastic quality of the work; the progress with some individuals is really precious and there are success stories in every single YIP,' she says.

Jo's background as a social worker, probation officer and youth worker has given her a good insight into the

different ways professionals engage with young people and the benefits of YIPs. 'The multi-agency strategy means that all the relevant agencies have a structured opportunity to identify the young people most in need of support, avoid duplication of services and share resources such as accommodation or staffing,' she explains.

Kickstart's manager David Williams feels that the approach works because of shared goals: 'It's not as difficult as it sounds to work with people from different agencies, because the outcomes still touch on each other,' he says. He gives the example of the tutorials, attended by youngsters like Mandy. 'Young people are getting an education and they are staying off the street and not committing crime, so the teachers are happy, the police are happy – everyone's happy.'

Personal approach
Richard Leahy runs the Kickstart tutorials. His background is in teaching, but he sees the benefit in working alongside other disciplines: 'As a teacher I'm always thinking about how the young person's education could be improved, whereas a youth worker will have a different viewpoint on how well a young person is doing because they see the other things that are going on in their lives.' But he adds that being open to a different mindset is a very personal thing, and that many traditional teachers would struggle in a YIP environment.

David Williams agrees that the success of multi-agency work is dependent on the individuals within the team: 'We're lucky that we have a fantastic police liaison officer and his attitude is more about trying to find out why that young person is getting involved in certain activities, rather than just to "nick 'em".'

Personalities aside, however, there's no escaping the fact that YIPs are tied up with crime reduction and the criminal justice system. Doesn't this put young people off and inhibit good youth work?

'Initially young people think you're associated with the police and they don't want to know, but once they see that this is actually a support mechanism, not about labelling them

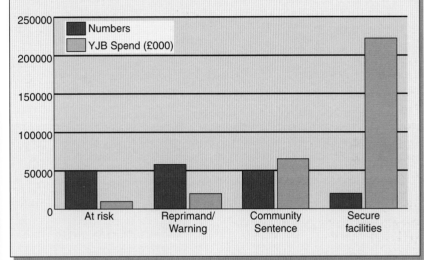

YIPs – a summary

YIPs target
A core group of 50 13- to 16-year-olds, who are identified as being most at risk of offending, truancy or school exclusion. YIPs aim to:
- Reduce arrests in the target group by 60%
- Reduce recorded crime in the area by 30%
- Achieve one-third reduction in truancy and exclusion in the target group
- Work for an average of 10 hours per week with each targeted young person

Why YIPs – economic justification
The Youth Justice Board estimates that a reduction of just 5% of what is spent on secure facilities would enable spending on prevention services for young people 'at risk' to be doubled (see chart below).

or trying to suppress them, they are fine,' says David.

Youth work and YIPs
Jo understands that some youth workers might feel uncomfortable in working alongside the criminal justice system, but she's quick to point out that all young people attending YIPs do so voluntarily, so the youth work itself isn't part of the system. She adds that YIPs differ from generic youth work and the approach is more akin to detached or street work.

'There are some kids, no matter how much work you do with them, they still go home every night, so, realistically, you can only help them with whatever difficulties they are going through

---

'There isn't a contradiction as long as there's a real understanding of the purpose, and people do it because they really want to work within that field,' she says.

It can be frustrating working with young people who are at risk of offending, says Richard. He gives an example of a young man who was doing very well in the tutorials. Then he simply stopped turning up, and Richard later discovered he'd been arrested for car theft. 'There are some kids, no matter how much work you do with them, they still go home every night, so, realistically, you can only help them with whatever difficulties they are going through, you can't guarantee you're going to be successful,' he says.

Government initiatives tend to generate paperwork, and YIPs are no exception. Richard says that the amount of administration is similar to that of a secondary school teacher. It's something he's used to, but he feels that it can hamper the quality of youth work. 'Some youth workers do find it taxing; the problem is that their skills are in youth work, not in filling out forms,' he says. David agrees: 'The form-filling is a bit of a nightmare,' he says.

Continued funding for a YIP is often dependent on a particular evaluation being completed on time. The problem for YIP managers like David is that critical information often comes from other sources, such as the police or social services. 'That's the downside of multi-agency work,' he explains. 'Although we have common goals, there are different priorities, and getting the right data at the right time always seems to be a problem.'

Younger YIPs?

However, the pen-pushing has a point, with evidence of success convincing policy-makers of YIPs' value. As a result, Junior YIPs are now being implemented, aimed at the 8-13 age group. These are running in Leicester and Leeds; ultimately there will be 60 nationwide. As with senior YIPs, funding has been promised until 2006.

The idea behind Junior YIPs is to help ease the 'key stage three dip', where children run into problems during the transition from primary to secondary school. They might include anything from a mentoring programme, after-school clubs and sports and arts projects, says Jo Burden: 'The key with junior YIPs is that they tackle the salient factors at a much younger stage. We're using evidence-based practice transferred

---

On the ground
What's it like for a YIP youth worker?

Naomi Hulston, 20, is a trainee youth worker with the Kickstart YIP in Southwark, London. Living locally, she has worked her way over the past two years from volunteer, through to working on sessional contracts and is now a full-time employee.

'In a typical day I'd come to work about 10 and then it would be PHSE, which is personal, health and social education for the year sevens in the local school. We run three-week workshops around drugs, racism, bullying and citizenship. Then I'd probably do some office-based work: some filing and letters. Throughout the day I might also be recruiting volunteers for the Junior Volunteer Awards or the Community Merit Awards, and doing a supervision here and there.

'Next I'd probably have a session, such as Soul Sisters (the young women's healthy living group Naomi created and runs for Kickstart) or a generic group or homework club at the school. The session would be from four onwards, 'til about eight-ish. The homework clubs came on board this year because we felt that when teaching PHSE the literacy levels of the year sevens was very poor and we wanted to set up groups to encourage them.

'This kind of work is forever changing. The most interesting aspect of my work over the past few weeks has been Soul Sisters, because we've been doing a video project about the area and their life. I've had very close contact with the Soul Sisters since I first set up the group in January this year. They're turning into lovely young women, whereas before they were kind of rough round the edges, very street.

'For me the biggest challenge of this job is timeframe, trying to stick to time and deadlines. I have lots of good ideas, but there aren't enough hours in the day, basically! But all the energy and time that we put in pays off. Seeing the young people raise their aspirations is the most rewarding part of my job. The opportunities for personal development are amazing.'

---

from an older age group, but it will be a case of finding out what people need and being very responsive to that.'

Further info

For more information on YIPs and junior YIPs: Crime Concern (runs junior and senior YIPs): www.crimeconcern.org.uk Youth Justice Board (funds senior YIPs): www.youth-justice-board.gov.uk The Children's Fund (funds junior YIPs): www.cypu.gov.uk/corporate/childrensfund UK government's crime reduction site: www.crimereduction.gov.uk *Understanding Anger* (£10.50) and *Facing Aggression* (£19.75) explore effective responses to angry and aggressive young people and are both available from UK Youth. Prices include p&p.

■ Clare Harvey is a freelance writer/journalist. Names have been changed.

■ The above information is from the magazine *UK Youth*, Autumn 2003, published by UK Youth and distributed to over 6,000 youth groups and youth workers. For further information visit their web site at www.ukyouth.org

© 2003 UK Youth

Young people in prison

Information from the Prison Reform Trust

Children in prison (under-18s)

- On 30 January 2004, there were 2,489 under-18-year-olds in prisons in England and Wales, almost exactly the same number as a year ago.
- The number of 15- to 17-year-olds in prison has nearly doubled over the last ten years.
- The Youth Justice Board failed to carry out its plan to remove all under-17-year-old girls from Prison Service accommodation during 2003. This is in line with a commitment originally given by the Home Office in March 1999 to place sentenced 15- and 16-year-old girls in available non-Prison Service accommodation.
- Reconviction rates are very high for children. In 1999, 80 per cent of 14- to 17-year-olds discharged from prison were reconvicted within two years,
- The majority of children in prison have been convicted of non-violent offences. In 2002, of the all boys in prison, just over a third were convicted of property crimes such as burglary and theft.
- Many children in prison have a background of severe social exclusion. Of those in custody of school age, over a quarter have literacy and numeracy levels of an average seven-year-old. Over half of those under 18 in custody have a history of being in care or social services involvement and studies have found that 45 per cent have been permanently excluded from school (Youth Justice Board statistics).
- Behavioural and mental health problems are particularly prevalent amongst children in prison. Of prisoners aged 16-20, around 85 per cent show signs of a personality disorder and 10 per cent exhibit signs of psychotic illness, for example schizophrenia (*Psychiatric Morbidity Among Young Offenders in England and Wales*, ONS, 2000).

- Drug and alcohol abuse are major problems. Of prisoners aged 16-20, over half reported dependence on a drug in the year prior to imprisonment. Over half the female and two-thirds of the male prisoners had a hazardous drinking habit prior to entering custody (*Psychiatric Morbidity Among Young Offenders in England and Wales*, ONS, 2000).
- The National Audit Office has highlighted the high number of movements of children between jails to make way for new arrivals, disrupting education and training courses and leading to inconsistent support and supervision. The NAO reports that there were 2,400 movements between April 2002 and January 2003.

Young people in prison (18-20-year-olds)

- On 30 January 2004, there were 10,645 under-21-year-olds in prisons in England and Wales. The vast majority, more than eight thousand, were aged 18-20.
- Young adult offenders (18- to 20-year-olds) make up 42 per cent of first-time offenders.
- Compared to other prisoners, young offenders are twice as likely to receive short-term sentences (less than 12 months). In 2002, short-term prisoners made up a quarter of the young adult prisoner population but nearly two-thirds of those received into prison in that year. The average time spent in custody for young adult prisoners serving less than 12 months is eight weeks and one day.
- The majority of young adults in prison have been convicted of non-violent offences. Of the young adult males who received custodial sentences in 2002, nearly a third were convicted of property crimes such as burglary and theft.
- Reconviction rates are particularly high for young people. In 1999, 71 per cent of young men released from prison were reconvicted within two years of release.
- Many young adult prisoners have a background of social exclusion. Nearly three-quarters were excluded from school at some stage, and 63 per cent were unemployed at the time of their arrest.
- Mental health problems, drug and alcohol abuse are common amongst young adult prisoners. Young adult prisoners are more likely than adults to suffer from mental health problems and are more likely to commit or attempt suicide than both younger and older prisoners.
- It is estimated that 25 per cent of young offenders are fathers while 39 per cent of female young offenders are mothers (HM Inspectorate of Prisons, *Young Prisoners: a thematic review, 1997*). Figures on the parenting status of prisoners are not routinely collected by the Home Office (Hansard, written answers, 28 April 2003).
- Young offender institutions and juvenile establishments have the highest assault rates of any prisons in England and Wales.
- The Chief Inspector of Prisons has expressed concern about the lack of a 'coherent national strategy, standards or new funding' for 18- to 21-year-olds despite a commitment in the 1997 Labour party manifesto to improve provision for this age group (*HM Chief Inspector of Prisons Annual Report, 2002-2003*).

■ The above information is from the Prison Reform Trust's web site: www.prisonreformtrust.org.uk

© Prison Reform Trust

Youth sentences and penalties

Information from the National Youth Agency

For some offences there is a fixed penalty or sentence (e.g. murder always results in a life sentence). In most cases, though, the magistrate or judge has a choice about what to do. You may receive an 'absolute discharge' which means that the court believes you are not guilty and you are free to go home. Alternatively if the court believes you are guilty of the crime you have been charged with, you may receive a 'custodial sentence'. You will either be sent to an adult prison or a young offender institution.

A custodial sentence is often given for very serious offences (e.g. murder, rape, armed robbery). For less serious offences the courts normally give another sentence. Anyone aged 10 or more can be given a custodial sentence but there are a lot of limits if you are under 18:

- People who are between the age of 10 and 17 can only be detained for long periods if they have committed one or more of the following crimes: indecent assault; causing death by dangerous driving; causing death while under the influence of drugs or drink; or an offence which carries at least a maximum sentence of 14 years' imprisonment for an adult (e.g. armed robbery).
- If you commit murder you can be detained until the Home Secretary decides it is safe to release you (which could be never).
- If you are 12-14 and have committed 3 or more offences of the sort an adult could go to prison for, you can be sentenced to a secure training order which means 6 months' to 2 years' punishment (half at a secure training centre and half in the community).
- If you are aged 15-17 then as well as long-term detention for very serious offences you can be

The National Youth Agency

sentenced to detention for other offences – like an adult except that you will go to a young offender institution for a maximum of 2 years.

What will my punishment be?

It depends on lots of things like whether you have a previous record, how serious the offence is, if you feel sorry for what you did and what level of punishment the court thinks is most effective.

If you are 17 or under and a community or custodial sentence seems likely the court will normally request a PSR (Pre-sentence report) which is a report made by a social worker or probation officer saying why you committed the offence and what can be done to stop or reduce the chance of you offending again.

The court uses the report to help it decide what sentence to impose.

Types of sentence

Absolute discharge
Although you are guilty, the offence is so minor that you will not be fined or punished in any way.

Conditional discharge
The court decides that although you are guilty you should be given a chance and so you are not punished there and then. However, if you commit another offence within a certain period of time, you may be punished for the first offence when you are sentenced for the second.

Binding over
You will be asked to sign a written promise that you will be of good behaviour for a certain period. If you are not you will be fined a maximum of £250 if you are under 14 and £1000 if you are under 18. If you are under 16 your parents rather than you can be bound over to make sure you behave. In some areas it is not the practice to bind over youth defendants.

Fine
You will be asked to pay a fixed sum according to how serious the offence was. The amounts are a maximum of £250 if you are under 14 and £1000 if you are under 18. If you are under 16 your parents rather than you will normally be asked to pay the fine.

Compensation order
If you have caused damage or injury to someone or their property, the court can order you to pay compensation to the victim, up to £5,000. This may be in addition to another sentence. The court should consider whether or not you are able to pay the amount. If you are under 16 your parents will normally be ordered to pay the sum. If you are under 17 they may be ordered to pay, although the court could also order that you pay it yourself.

Community sentence
Sentences of this kind are orders by the court for you to attend a centre, carry out community work or begin a

period of guidance or supervision with a probation officer or social worker. Details of the order will depend on the seriousness of the offence you committed and whether or not a suitable centre or programme is available. If you do not obey the order you can be brought back to court and sentenced in some other way.

Combination orders

Community sentences can be called attendance sentence orders, supervision orders, probation orders or community service orders. You can be sentenced to a community service order and a probation order at the same time. This is known as a combination order.

Custodial sentence

This means that you will be held somewhere secure like a young offender institution or a prison. You cannot be sent to an adult prison unless you are over 21. If you are between 15 and 21 years old you will be sent to a young offender institution. To be given a custodial sentence you must have committed a serious crime. Or it may be that you are a danger to the public. If you refuse to do a community sentence you may also be given a custodial sentence. The Youth Court does not have the power to send you to an adult prison, although it can sentence you to a period in a young offender institution up to six months for one offence (12 months for two or more offences). If the Youth Court feels that you should get a longer sentence it can send you to the Crown Court for sentencing.

Exclusion order

This is usually used for offences relating to football matches. If you are violent or found drinking alcohol at a match where it is banned, the court can prevent you from attending further matches. An exclusion order is given as an additional sentence on top of another one. The sentence might be for a public order offence like violence, racial harassment or drunk and disorderly conduct.

Deferred sentence

A sentence may be postponed if there are major changes for the better in your life and the court thinks you should be given the opportunity to show that these changes are going to last.

Secure training order

A sentence to a period in a secure training centre followed by a period of supervision.

Secure remands

This is where you go to live in local authority accommodation but with a condition about security (e.g. limits on when you can go out). This is being introduced as an option for the court in sentencing 12- to 16-year-olds.

Curfew orders

A curfew order is where you are required to stay in a certain place at certain time (e.g. in your home after 10 at night). Curfews can be for between 2 and 12 hours a day and they can last for up to six months.

Electronic monitoring

Electronic monitoring is sometimes called 'electronic tagging' or 'tagging'. Tagging is where an electronic device is put on you to monitor where you are. It is quite likely to be used in combination with a curfew; to check that you are following the curfew. Tagging has been viewed by some people as a breach of civil rights. However, it can be used to improve rights – for instance the Labour government is considering using tagging as an alternative to custody (e.g. prison) in some cases where a person is not dangerous.

Binding over parents

This sounds a bit like your parents getting tied up if you commit an offence! Actually it is where the court orders your parent(s)/guardian(s) to take care of and exercise control over you and make sure you carry out your community sentence properly. If they don't do this they will have to forfeit up to £1000!

■ The above information is from the National Youth Agency's Youth Information web site: www.youthinformation.com Alternatively, see page 41 for their address details.

© *National Youth Agency (NYA)*

Busy doing nothing

The experience of 18- to 20-year-old men on remand

New research published 4 November 2003 by the Howard League for Penal Reform shows that remanding more than 8,000 young men aged 18 to 20 to prison every year is wasteful and unproductive. The report *Busy Doing Nothing: the experience of 18- to 20-year-old men on remand* exposes the multiple problems and needs of these young people and contrasts this to the impoverished daily life in prison.

The report reveals that the overwhelming majority of the remanded young men are only held in prison for a short time and yet very little is done to address their problems, leading to disrupted lives and more crime. The Howard League for Penal Reform concludes that custodial remands should be reduced and that regimes should be improved to provide education and training.

The research shows that 18- to 20-year-old men in prison are an extremely needy group. Like all young people of this age it is a time of transition, of maturation, with increasing independence, responsibility and decision-making for the future. Yet the prison system provides little specialist help. The research was based on individual interviews with prison staff and prisoners and a literature search of the existing research and found that:

- Drugs. 9 out of 10 young prisoners admit to having used drugs. All of the young men we spoke with agreed that drugs and alcohol had played a part in their lives prior to imprisonment.
- No job. Research shows that only a third had work when they were arrested. Of those young men we spoke to who had worked said it was boring, working in factories or in the building trade.
- A desire for money.

The report shows a prison experience which is characterised by inactivity in their cells. One young man commented that 'I can tell you every single programme that is on [TV] during the day . . . I want to do something other than sleep and eat.' They were bored, lethargic and lacked any foresight about their future. But they were not complacent about their experience of prison and spoke about wanting to use this time to build for their futures.

The overwhelming majority of the remanded young men are only held in prison for a short time and yet very little is done to address their problems

---

The report challenges the prison service to develop its services and regime for this group. The uncertain, often short and disrupted time in prison through court appearances is no excuse for inactivity or not using resources creatively. The Howard League for Penal Reform suggests that a different approach to service provision is adopted using more wing-based activities with modular programmes delivered via a rolling programme to address the clearly identified needs of the young men, and help them enhance their prospect of positive futures on release.

Anita Dockley, author of the report, said

'The Howard League for Penal Reform is acutely aware that the needs and problems of young men aged 18-20 in the prison system are not being dealt with adequately. They have not received the same amount of attention as other prisoners. They can no longer be neglected.

'The problems facing young men on remand are particularly pressing. They need support and guidance during a period when their lives are changing and they are expected to take on the responsibilities of adulthood. But as remand prisoners with uncertain and often short periods in prison they are not being enabled to even take opportunities that may be available to other prisoners.

'The prison system has to understand the needs of this age group and rise to the challenge of creating a different way of providing access to services, information and help despite the uncertainty of imprisonment on remand. There can be no excuse for inactivity.'

Kim Morgan, from the Persula Foundation, added, 'The Persula Foundation has worked for several years in the field of criminal justice and is keen to support the work being undertaken by the Howard League. We have been focusing on the field of remand prisoners recently as a fundamental issue of human rights, as well as part of the issue of penal reform, and as such are very pleased to have been part of the process of creating this report.'

- The above information is from the Howard League for Penal Reform's web site which can be found at www.howardleague.org

Girls inside

Lorraine Atkinson reports on how a Howard League project is highlighting the urgent need for the government to fulfil its promises not to place girls in prison

Among the 110 girls under 18 currently held in prison, Claire would pass unnoticed. She is 16, pale and very small for her age. She is serving an eight-month prison sentence for deception. She told the Howard League she had collected £300 in sponsorship money from her neighbours which she then spent on crack cocaine. When Claire arrived at the prison she had only one set of clothes and a toothbrush in a polythene bag.

She has been through the care system. She began drinking at 13 years old and by the age of 16 was using crack cocaine. She was living in poverty with little support from her family. Like the majority of girls in prison she is damaged and highly vulnerable.

The Youth Justice Board has promised to remove girls under 17 years old from prison custody by the end of 2003. This is not the first time however that promises have been made to take vulnerable girls like Claire out of prison. In 1999, following Howard League research and a campaign to remove girls from prison, the then home secretary, Jack Straw, announced that 15- and 16-year-old girls would be placed in local authority care, not in prison. The government promised that in the longer term, sentenced young women aged 17 would also be placed outside Prison Service custody. In March 2001, the Youth Justice Board stated it was an absolute priority to place all young women outside adult prisons by mid 2002.

Despite such promises, girls continued to be placed in prison. In October 2002 there were 110 girls in prison, 7 aged 15, 19 aged 16 and 84 aged 17. In fact, the number of girls aged under 18 in prison has risen by 28 per cent, from 86 in 1999 to 110 in 2002. Contrary to popular perceptions, however, girls are not committing more crimes. The number of girls aged 15-17 found guilty or cautioned for all offences has dropped from 22,900 in 1998 to 21,200 in 2000.

Reports by the Prisons Inspectorate have repeatedly highlighted the fact that prison is an unsuitable environment for teenage girls. In October 2001, inspectors at Eastwood Park Prison noted: 'It was impossible not to be struck by the profound personality disturbance and mental health problems that many presented and by the inappropriateness of prison, or indeed any other custodial placement for them.'

Girls in prison often feel cut off from their families and for many of them it is their first time away from home

---

An inspection of Holloway prison in July 2002 raised serious concerns about the small number of girls held in Holloway, so serious in fact that the chief inspector of prisons, Anne Owers, immediately contacted Martin Nairey, the director-general of the Prison Service, and Lord Warner, chairman of the Youth Justice Board, to request urgent action.

While we wait for the government and the Youth Justice Board to act on their promises to remove girls from prison, the Howard League has set up a project to offer support and provide an advocacy service for girls under 18 years old in prison. The Howard League project has supported girls like Carmel, who is 17 years old. She left home at the age of 15 as her mother used to beat her up and had been living on the streets for two years, sharing a squat and even sleeping in a tent. Carmel had no money and no clothes apart from those lent to her by the prison so the Howard League bought her clothes and books. Carmel had previously had a mentor who had been supporting her, but had lost touch. The Howard League was able to trace her mentor and inform them of Carmel's whereabouts.

The project has also offered continuing emotional support to Charlotte who was finding it increasingly difficult to cope in prison. Charlotte was 17 years old and had served five months of her 15-month sentence for street robbery. She said she had had enough of prison and had been put on anti-depressants by healthcare staff. She told the Howard League weekends were the worst time for her: 'There's nothing to do in here at the weekend. You are locked in your cell and you just think about things all the time. If I was at home, I'd talk to my mum if I was worried about something but you can't do that in prison, can you?'

In desperation, Charlotte took a glass jar, smashed it and cut her arms with the broken glass. Charlotte said she had never injured herself before she came to prison but she had seen other girls doing it. She was extremely ashamed of cutting herself and said she would never do it again. However, she cut herself again a couple of weeks later when faced with a crisis at home.

Over half the girls referred to the project have asked for help with a family problem. Girls in prison often feel cut off from their families and for many of them it is their first time away from home. Girls are often a long way from their parents or carers and visits can be difficult, or even impossible. Girls have limited access to the telephone in prison and for some the only contact they have is by post.

Samantha is 17 years old and serving an 18-month sentence for affray. While she was in prison her mother died. Samantha was devastated and kept saying: 'I can't believe it has happened, it feels like a dream.' She blamed herself for her mother's death. At a time when she really needed her family around her, to share in her grief, Samantha was over 100 miles away, locked in a prison with limited access to the telephone and few close friends to turn to. The Howard League was able to support Samantha in a practical way, by buying clothes for her to wear at the funeral and by talking to her family about her possessions. Samantha not only lost her mother but also her family home as she was too young to take it on herself.

Bullying is another common issue raised by girls referred to the project. Bridget was an extremely vulnerable 17-year-old with learning

Young offenders in prison

Prison population as at 20/2/2004

Population 20/2/2004	74,594
Population on corresponding Friday 2003	71,986
Yearly change	+ 2,608
Adult Males	59,812
Young Offenders[1] – Male	10,310
Adult Females	3,958
Young Offenders[1] – Female	514

1. A young offender is defined as someone who is aged between 15 and 21 years of age inclusive.

Source: HM Prison Service, Crown copyright

difficulties. She said that she was being bullied by a group of girls on the wing and she had burn marks where cigarettes had been stubbed out on her arm. She said other girls had stolen her tobacco. Bridget felt unable to cope with the bullying and was in tears as she described her experiences. She threatened to harm herself if it continued.

The Howard League talked to prison staff about Bridget and a suicide and self-harm form was opened, which meant she would be regularly monitored. Staff were also extremely worried about Bridget but

felt unable to meet her complex needs. As one officer said: 'She needs someone to watch her all the time but we can't do that here.' The ratio of prison staff to prisoners is low and often there are just one or two officers to deal with the needs of 30 girls.

Girls in prison represent some of the most damaged and vulnerable young people. Over half the girls the Howard League has worked with say they have experienced family breakdown and six had been homeless. Nearly half the girls admitted to having a drug and alcohol problem. Six girls have disclosed physical and sexual abuse in the past, although the actual figure is probably much higher than this.

The Howard League continues to argue that prison is not and never will be a suitable environment for teenage girls. Prison can only serve to have a brutalising and even more damaging effect on them and the sooner promises to remove all girls under 18 from prison are fulfilled, the better.

■ Lorraine Atkinson is policy officer at the Howard League for Penal Reform.

■ The above article first appeared in *YoungMinds* magazine Issue 63. Visit their web site at www.youngminds.org.uk

© *YoungMinds*

Girls in prisons

Girls held in adult prisons against their 'best interests'

In a high court decision today a judge held that holding a 16-year-old girl in an adult prison was not in her 'best interests' as required under Human Rights law but because the Government had not provided enough places in secure children's homes he could not find it unlawful.

The case was taken by the Howard League for Penal Reform on behalf of 'DT', a 16-year-old girl, who was incarcerated at Eastwood Park women's prison.

In his judgment Mr Justice Hooper said: 'It is difficult to see how

it can be said to be in the best interests of a 16-year-old, such as the claimant, to spend a considerable amount of time on association with those 18 and over.'

He also said that her move to an adult prison from a secure children's home would breach the UN Convention on the Rights of the Child but for the fact that the Government has entered a reservation saying it is unable to abide by the Convention and keep juveniles separate from adults in the penal system.

The court had heard evidence from the girl how in prison she came across drugs and women so distressed they were cutting themselves and some attempted suicide. She said, 'You can hear staff asking for scissors to cut people down' and 'in prison you are locked up for long periods of time and there is no time to get to know the staff'.

Her evidence was corroborated by a report on the prison made by the Chief Inspector of Prisons Anne Owers who said that girls seriously cutting themselves or being found unconscious with a ligature was almost a daily experience.

The report also said that there were no separate facilities for the under-18s who mixed with adults. It commented on the 'inappropriateness of prison' for these girls, many of whom had 'profound personality disturbance and mental health problems'

However in the judgment on the case taken by the Howard League for Penal Reform the judge said that as a matter of law the shortage of places in the system meant that it was lawful to put the girl in prison despite these conditions.

In the evidence presented on behalf of the Government it was acknowledged that in 1999 the Government had given a commitment to remove all girls from the prison system because it was not in their best interests to place them there. They had failed to do this because they had not provided enough places in secure children's homes and secure training centres which all acknowledge are better equipped to deal with children.

Putting such children in prison will only ensure there is a greater chance they will offend again and does nothing to rehabilitate them

---

Speaking today Frances Crook, Director of the Howard League, said: 'This judgment is essentially saying that putting children in prison with adults might be lawful but it is not right. The judge accepted entirely our evidence that girls are still held in adult prisons because the Govern-ment has failed to adequately fund facilities suitable for holding children. Putting such children in prison will only ensure there is a greater chance they will offend again and does nothing to re-habilitate them.

'This is yet another judge saying that prison is a damaging place for children at a time when David Blunkett is reducing the number of places in secure chil-drens homes. We call on him to reverse this decision.'

The Howard League is considering an appeal.

■ On 20 January 2004 there were 68 girls under the age of 18 held in prison service accommodation.

■ The above information is from the Howard League for Penal Reform's web site which can be found at www.howardleague.org
© The Howard League for Penal Reform

Criminal responsibility

Information from www.learn.co.uk

What is criminal responsibility?

The age of criminal responsibility means the age at which a person can be prosecuted for a crime. It should be the age at which they understand the consequences of a crime and take full responsibility for that crime.

At what age do you think a child or young person is old enough to stand trial?

The age of criminal respons-ibility varies from country to country.

This table shows the age within some European countries.

Country	Age of criminal responsibility
Luxembourg	18
Spain	16
Denmark	15
Holland	13
England, Wales and Northern Ireland	10
Scotland	8

As you can see, in England, Wales and Northern Ireland children can be prosecuted from the age of 10, but from country to country it varies a great deal. This should tell you that people disagree about what is the right age to set for criminal respons-ibility.

Here are two differing views about the age of criminal respons-ibility. The first argues for raising the age from 10 years to 14 years, while the other thinks the age should be reduced to 8 years old. Read them carefully and see if you can pick out some of the issues.

The age of criminal responsibility means the age at which a person can be prosecuted for a crime

---

Carolyn Hamilton Director, Children's Legal Centre
I would say about 14. I think that at that age children are better able to understand the consequences of what they are doing. A child of 10 who has committed an offence is more appropriately dealt with in the care system than in the criminal justice system. The European court says that a child must be able to participate in their own defence and I think a child of 14 is able to do that. The Committee on the Rights of the Child has said that 10 is too young for criminal responsibility. If our aim is rehabilitation, it is best done under the civil system, not the criminal justice system.

(Source: The Panel, the Guardian, 20 June 2002, interviews by Diane Taylor)

Lyn Costello, Mothers Against Murder and Aggression
Children of 10 know the difference between right and wrong. They know

you don't hurt small children. Any parent will tell you there are cases where children play rough and get hurt, but they know it's wrong to kill a child . . . We have children as young as eight, or even six, terrorising people on estates such as the one I live on. I also think parents should be held responsible for their children's behaviour . . .

(Source: The Panel, the *Guardian*, 20 June 2002, interviews by Diane Taylor)

Here are some of the issues that these two people consider:

- Do children know what they are doing?
- Do they understand the consequences (results) of what they are doing?
- Should children be dealt with by the care system or the criminal system?
- Is a child able to participate in his or her own defence?
- Do we want to punish or to rehabilitate children?
- Should parents be responsible for their child's behaviour?

It is a complex issue. As you consider how you feel about it, you might think of your own experiences of children and young people, and when you think it's right for them to take complete responsibility for criminal actions. You might also consider when the law gives children and young people responsibilities in other areas, such as alcohol, marriage and driving.

What is the youth justice system?

Young people may be tried for a crime as young as 10, but the youth justice system means that in many ways they will be treated differently from an adult. So what are the differences?

Well, imagine that you are a juvenile (between 10 and 17) and you have been arrested. Follow the steps to see what you may experience.

1. The police station
When you arrive at the police station, the duty officer must find an appropriate adult to advise and assist you.

This will usually be your parent, guardian, care worker, social worker

or whoever has responsibility for your welfare. This adult must be present when you are:

- informed of your rights
- searched
- involved in an identification procedure, such as an ID parade
- interviewed
- charged with an offence.

S/he may also instruct a solicitor on your behalf and speak with you privately at any time.

2. The youth court
As you are under 18, your case will begin in a youth court. This is usually a magistrates' court which you will probably find less overwhelming and intimidating than a crown court. Only if the offence is very serious will it go to a crown court.

Because you are in a youth court they will change some of the proceedings to help you understand what is happening and to be more supportive. These changes should include:

- allowing your parent or guardian to sit close to you
- you will be addressed by your first name

Young people may be tried for a crime as young as 10, but the youth justice system means that in many ways they will be treated differently from an adult

---

- witnesses and barristers will be asked to use language that you will understand
- in a crown court, the judge and barristers will not wear wigs
- reporting restrictions will prevent press publicity.

3. Sentencing
If the magistrate finds you not guilty, then you will walk free from the court. If you are found guilty, the magistrate has a range of penalties to choose from. Some of the penalties or punishments are different from those given to adult prisoners.

The youth justice system wants to prevent you from offending again, by using measures which are designed to keep you out of trouble. Here are some of the possible sentences:

Supervision orders: this means you will be put under the supervision of a probation officer or a member of a youth offending team, with sessions and courses to attend.

Parenting orders: if you are under 16, your parents may have to attend classes to help make sure you don't get into any more trouble

Curfew orders: such an order will usually confine you to home for part of the day (if you are over 16).

Community service orders: these require offenders (over 16) to undertake some part-time work for the benefit of the community.

Custodial sentence: this may mean a detention and training order if you are between 12 and 17, or time in a young offender institution if you are between 18 and 21.

© *Content courtesy of Learnthings Ltd*

Staying safe

Personal safety

The chance that you or a member of your family will be a victim of violent crime is low. However, many people are still frightened that they, or someone close to them, will be the victim of a violent attack.

There are sensible precautions you can take to cut the risk of attack. This article provides simple and effective advice for both men and women, which can help you stay safe.

At home . . .

- make sure your home is secure (see the National Neighbourhood Watch Association *Home Security* factsheet for tips on keeping your home safe)
- if you are moving don't show tenants or buyers around the house on your own
- draw your curtains after dark
- if you see signs of a break-in at home, don't go in, the intruder may still be there – go to a neighbour's and call the police.

Out and about

If you are often out and about on your own or in the dark then there are lots of simple precautions you can take to keep yourself safe:

- carry a personal attack alarm. These are available from DIY stores and often from local police. It is a good idea to carry the alarm in your hand so you can use it immediately to scare off an attacker
- if you are carrying a bag, keep it close to you with clasps and zips inwards
- keep house keys in your pocket so that if your bag is stolen, a thief won't have your house keys and your address
- if you think somebody may be following you, check by crossing the street once or twice to see if

they follow you. If it seems that they are, or you are still worried then go to the nearest place with people, such as a pub or shop and call the police. Avoid using a phonebox in the street as an attacker may try and trap you inside

- if you follow the same route regularly then it is a good idea to change your route from time to time
- always stick to well-lit areas
- on parks and commons keep to the main paths and open spaces – avoid wooded areas
- if you are wearing a personal stereo remember that you cannot hear traffic or somebody approaching behind you
- don't take short cuts through dark alleys

- walk facing the traffic so a car can't pull up behind you
- don't hitch-hike or take lifts from strangers
- cover up expensive-looking jewellery and keep mobile phones and wallets/purses hidden away
- at cash machines don't let anyone see your personal identity number.

Staying safe in taxis

- if you are going to be out late, try to arrange a lift home or book a taxi through a registered company
- check that the taxi that arrives is the one that you ordered
- when you get home a taxi driver can help you by waiting until you are safely inside before he drives off
- do not hail minicabs from the street or use taxis that are touting for trade – this is not only illegal, but you also have no guarantee that the driver is licensed
- do not sit in the front seat of the taxi – always sit in the back
- if you feel uneasy, ask to be let out in a well-lit area where there are plenty of people
- if in any doubt, don't get in a taxi.

Public transport

- try to stay away from isolated bus stops, especially after dark
- on an empty bus, sit near the driver or conductor
- on a train sit in a compartment with lots of other people and check to see where the emergency chain is.

Mobile phone theft

Mobile phone theft is on the increase and thousands of phones are stolen by street robbers every month. To prevent being a victim of mobile phone theft you should:

- try not to use your phone in crowded areas where someone could easily snatch it from you
- avoid keeping your phone in public view.

In case your phone is stolen you should keep a safe record of the following details – these will help to trace your phone and make it more difficult for thieves to use it and sell it on:

- always use your phone's security pin code
- security mark the battery and phone with your postcode (UV pens are available from your local police station or DIY stores)
- register your phone with your network operator – they will then be able to block your phone's SIM card if it is stolen
- make a note of the serial number of your handset – you can get this by typing *#06# into your phone. This number is unique to your handset. If your phone is stolen, this number will enable your phone manufacturer to block the actual phone handset.

If you follow all of these precautions your phone will be effectively useless to thieves making them less attractive to steal.

Car jacking

Car jacking is not necessarily a new form of crime, but like mobile phone crime, it is on the increase. Take these simple steps to protect yourself:

- keep car doors locked while you are driving around town
- keep valuables such as bags and mobile phones out of sight
- try to park in well-lit areas where there are other people around
- when you return to your car have your keys ready so you can get straight in
- never give lifts to strangers
- if another car tries to signal you to stop or you think you are being followed then drive to a busy place such as a garage or even a police station before stopping. Even then keep your doors locked until you are sure there is no danger
- never leave keys in the ignition when you are out of your car
- if bumped from behind stay in your car with the doors locked and wait for the other driver to approach you. If you are suspicious then ask the driver to follow you to your local police station
- if you feel threatened then use your lights, horn and mobile phone to summon help.

Remember your safety is more important than your property – if somebody attempts to snatch your bag, phone or car, then the safest thing to do is to let it go.

- The above information is from a factsheet produced by the National Neighbourhood Watch Association®. For further information visit their web site which can be found at www.neighbourhoodwatch.net

© National Neighbourhood Watch Association®

Police numbers reach record

By Alan Travis, Home Affairs Editor

Police numbers in England and Wales have reached a new all-time high of 138,155 – and are rising at the rate of 6,000 every year. The latest Home Office figures for December 2003 published 2 March 2004 show that the number of police officers reached its highest level since records began in 1921.

Police numbers in England and Wales fell for the first two years of the Labour government dipping to 132,000 in 1999 but have steadily increased every year since then after ministers introduced a ringfenced 'crime fighting fund' to ensure that chief constables did not use the money for other purposes.

Police strengths have also been supplemented by the recruitment of 3,243 community support officers by the end of February 2004 working in 38 police forces. They are paid less than uniformed constables but have limited powers to stop and detain and issue fixed penalty notices.

The home secretary, David Blunkett, said: 'Police numbers continue to rise and it is vital that we make the best use of them to make a real difference to the quality of life in our communities. I want to build on the progress we have already made by redefining the relationship of the police with the people they serve, making them locally accountable and more responsive to local needs.'

Some senior police officers have recently criticised the flow of government funding for extra officers, arguing that simply providing more bodies was distorting police priorities. It is expected that the annual increase in police numbers will now begin to slow down with only 650 extra being recruited in this financial year.

Commenting on the growing number of CSOs, a Home Office spokeswoman said: 'This is not policing on the cheap, but an additional resource over and above record police numbers. They perform a separate but complementary role to police officers in patrolling streets and tackling anti-social behaviour.'

© Guardian Newspapers Limited 2004

Youth justice

Information from the National Youth Agency

Reducing youth crime and reforming the youth justice system are a major part of the Government's effort to build safer communities and tackle social exclusion. Recently the Government has begun the most radical reform of the youth justice system for 50 years. Reforms aim to prevent offending by children and young people, by:

- developing a clear strategy to prevent offending and re-offending by children and young people;
- helping offenders, and their parents, to face up to their offending behaviour and take responsibility for their actions;
- earlier, more effective intervention when young people first offend;
- faster, more efficient procedures from arrest to sentence; and
- partnership between all youth justice agencies to deliver a better, faster system.

The Crime and Disorder Act 1998 established preventing offending as the principal aim of the youth justice system.

Tackling youth crime

The Crime and Disorder Act provides a range of new measures designed to help local communities and youth justice agencies take effective action to tackle youth crime. These include:

- local child curfew schemes to protect children under the age of 10 in a particular area from getting into trouble. Under these powers, which were brought into force on 30 September 1998, local authorities may apply to the Home Office to establish a local scheme which may, for example, form part of local crime and disorder strategies required under section 6 of the Act;
- child safety order to provide targeted intervention with children under 10 at risk of getting into trouble;
- anti-social behaviour orders to

The National Youth Agency

deal with serious, but not necessarily criminal, anti-social behaviour by those aged 10 and above. These powers were brought into force on 1 April 1999; and
- powers for the police to remove truants to designated premises to allow the police, working with local authorities and schools, to tackle truancy, one of the factors that put young people at risk of offending. These powers came into force on 1 December 1998.

The Crime and Disorder Act 1998 established preventing offending as the principal aim of the youth justice system

---

The Act also includes powers for the police and courts to intervene when young people do offend. This may be through:

- final warning schemes to replace police cautioning of young offenders;
- reparation order requiring young offenders to make amends to their victim or the wider community;

- action plan order to tackle offending behaviour and its causes;
- parenting order to help reinforce and support parental responsibility (a parenting order may also be used in combination with an anti-social behaviour order or a child safety order);
- drug treatment and testing order for convicted offenders aged 16 and over whose crimes are connected to funding their drug habit. This is an alternative to a custodial sentence if the offender agrees to a programme of regular testing and treatment; and
- court ordered secure remands – to hold certain alleged offenders in local authority secure accommodation while they await their trial.

New structures at local and national level have been introduced to provide the framework to tackle youth offending. Youth offending teams will bring together the staff and wider resources of the police, social services, the probation service, education and health, in the delivery of youth justice services, with the scope to involve others, including the voluntary sector.

At national level, the Youth Justice Board for England and Wales, which began operation on 30 September 1998, will provide oversight of the operation of the teams and the youth justice system as a whole.

Youth Offending Teams – previously Social Services departments, work with Social Services, Police, probation, education departments and health authorities to achieve their statutory responsibility to prevent and ensure effective diversions from offending.

- The above information is from the National Youth Agency's Youth Information web site: www.youthinformation.com

Alternatives to custody

Information from www.crimeinfo.org.uk

The basics

Prison is not the only sentence available to judges and magistrates deciding on how to punish an offender. Only a minority of people found guilty of crimes are sent to prison, most are given a community sentence. These are run by the Probation Service and are characterised by either a 'payback' element (such as paying a fine or working unpaid for the community), or 'rehabilitation', changing an offender's views and lifestyle to prevent them committing more crimes in the future.

Inside information

The main community penalties are:

Community rehabilitation order

Those on a community rehabilitation order are supervised by a probation officer. The order may also require the offender to participate in offending behaviour programmes, such as alcohol and driving, anger management and domestic violence programmes. There, they face up to their crimes, the damage they've caused and the changes they need to make to their lives.

Community punishment order

Offenders have to do unpaid work that benefits the community. Canals are dredged, graveyards are cleared, village halls are renovated, playgrounds are created, cycle paths are constructed, mosques are painted, etc.

Did you know?

Over a million fines are imposed every year. The money collected goes to the Treasury.

About 8 million hours of work are contributed to local communities each year through community service carried out on these orders.

---

the Centre for Crime and Justice Studies

Community punishment and rehabilitation order

The order combines the main elements of community rehabilitation orders and community punishment orders, so it involves unpaid community work as well as supervision by a probation officer, and sometimes participation in an offending behaviour programme.

Other alternatives to custody

Curfew order

This is a form of 'house arrest'. Monitoring takes place through an electronic tag worn on the ankle. The court specifies which hours the offender has to be at home (which can be between 2 and 12 hours a day), and how long the order lasts (anything up to six months). In the hours when the offender is supposed to be at home, the tag sends a signal down a phone line to a control centre. If the offender goes out, the signal is broken and the control centre is alerted. The offender may then be taken back to court for breaching the order.

Drug treatment and testing order

This order is targeted at people who commit crime to fund their drugs habit. Offenders are treated for their addiction and must undergo frequent tests to prove that they are responding to the treatment and not continuing to use drugs. Every month the offender goes back to court for their progress to be reviewed.

Fine

Fines are the most frequently used court order. The offender has to pay an amount of money decided by the court; if they can't pay immediately, they can arrange to pay weekly. If the offender fails to make payments, they can be punished, and even sent to prison.

Compensation order

Like the fine, but here the money is used to compensate the victim when the crime has involved personal injury or loss. Compensation orders are usually made alongside other sentences, such as community rehabilitation orders or community punishment.

Attendance centre order

This is only for 10- to 21-year-olds, and requires attendance at a special centre for between 12 and 36 hours in total. Attendance centres are run by the police and are usually open on Saturdays. While they are there offenders often take part in a range of activities designed to work on their offending behaviour.

Discharge

There are two types of discharge – absolute and conditional. Absolute has no conditions attached and is used when the court feels that no further action is required. It may be that the offence was very minor and out of character, or it might be that the whole experience of arrest and the court appearance has had a major effect.

A conditional discharge is made for a period of time – anything up to three years. This means that there will be no further action as long as the offender does not commit another offence during that time. If they do commit another offence, then as well as a sentence for the new offence, the court can also re-sentence the offender for the original offence.

■ The above information is from the web site www.crimeinfo.org.uk

© *Centre for Crime and Justice Studies (CCJS)*

How to help tackle young people causing problems

Information from Crime Concern

Introduction

We've all seen young people hanging around, whether it's at the bus stop, outside the local shops or in the park. Most of the time, they are well behaved, but their high spirits may lead to rowdiness, and to some adults and children this can feel threatening.

Sometimes young people do behave violently or commit other crimes, and this is not acceptable. At the same time, young people are most likely to be victims of crime, and can be at risk when they hang around. Many of them are also just as unhappy as adults about crime issues. But what can we do? This article looks at some ways to tackle problems with young people in your community.

How are young people causing a problem in your area?

Many people confuse youth presence with youth nuisance. Young people can seem threatening, but may just be larking about. Like anyone else, young people are capable of a wide range of behaviour. Most of them are probably law abiding, and just exhibiting high spirits. Others may commit serious crimes, be extremely anti-social and abuse or intimidate people.

There are things you need to know to help you understand the problem with young people in your area. One of the best ways to gather this information, and to get young people involved, is to ask the young people to collect the information themselves. They'll need to ask the following questions:

Q. Where do young people hang out? Is it outside a shop, in the park, by a bus stop?

Q. What are they doing? Are they just hanging around? Are they playing games or music? Are they drinking or taking drugs? Are they deliberately intimidating people?

CR!ME CONCERN
WORKING FOR SAFER COMMUNITIES

Q. When do they do this? Is it day or night time? Is it worse in school holidays, or at weekends? What days are worst?

Q. What else is there for them to do? Is there a youth club? If so, when is it open?

Particular problems

Graffiti, vandalism and criminal damage

Young people are blamed for most graffiti, vandalism and criminal damage.

What can we do?

■ Clean graffiti up immediately – and keep cleaning it up. Your council's Environmental Health Department may well have a policy on this. They may be able to support you in setting up a 'rapid removal squad' or be willing to target a specific 'hot-spot' area which you have identified.

■ Community arts projects, where members of the community work with an artist, can improve public spaces and give young people pride or a stake in their surroundings. This can also be a good way to get people from different generations working together.

Underage drinking

If young people are rowdy when they hang around anyway, alcohol is only going to make the situation worse. There is a lot of pressure on young people to drink, from their peers, and from society as a whole, but underage drinking is illegal. It is also illegal for shops to sell alcohol to someone underage.

Good practice

Working with police, schools and local vendors, one county council established a 'Responsible Vendor' scheme to help cut down the amount of underage drinking. Young people receive proof-of-age cards, and vendors make sure these are checked. In this way, the whole community worked together to tackle underage drinking.

What can we do?

■ Police and Environmental Health Officers at the council

ISN'T IT BETTER TO BE *HANGIN'* IN HERE THAN *HANGIN' OUT* THERE?

YOUTH ART EXHIBIT

CREATED BY SKEET, KAZ + SHO

should ensure that shopkeepers are not selling alcohol to young people. Ask the police what they are doing to enforce this, and ask them to report on progress to you.

■ Make sure young people know the health risks of drinking. Help them learn to say no to their peers, and to find different ways to spend their time.

Hanging about

On the one hand, young people have always 'hung around'. On the other hand, this can seem very intimidating, even if the young people are not causing trouble.

Good practice

Young people in a town in Wales worked with older people to share worries and get to know one another. This scheme started when one lady was invited into the school to meet some young people. This brought home to young people that their actions were sometimes seen as intimidating, and encouraged them to take responsibility for this. Older members of the community also got to know some young people and to see them as individuals, not as a threat.

What can we do?

Ask young people what they would like to be doing, and help them to do it. Some things which young people have set up in other areas have included:

■ skate parks
■ youth shelters
■ Help develop more provision at existing youth clubs, or the development of new ones, for example, using school buildings or existing facilities out-of-hours.

Abuse and intimidation

Some young people do commit crimes, behave extremely anti-socially and terrorise their neighbourhoods. This problem can be made worse by the police seemingly not doing anything about it.

What can we do?

■ If you have done some work to find out more about the problem, you can tell the police about this. They may be able to target their policing to times when the problem is at its worst.

■ To help the police use their time as effectively as possible, you could produce a leaflet to give to local people explaining when the police should be called, and what they can do.

■ You can also encourage people to keep a record of criminal behaviour by young people. This may help the police if the person goes to court.

What else can we do?

Mentoring, mediation and community conferencing all involve adults working with young people to resolve differences and disputes, whether they are between individuals, groups or generations. All of these things will get adults and young people working together for common goals, as well as helping people to develop new skills.

It is important to include young people in planning. Ask them what they want, support them in their decisions, and allow them to take the lead on projects.

Other things you can do

■ Support peer consultation, where young people are trained to find out what other young people think, and to represent this to the rest of the community.

■ Improve communications, for example 'Question Time' between young and older people. Even just having two generations using a facility at the same time can have positive effects for inter-generational understanding.

■ Support young people in setting up their own tenants and residents' groups.

Who else can help?

Your local council – especially Youth Services. Local schools.

■ If you have a bright idea on how police services could be improved in your area, tell us and you could be in for a reward! Come to our website at www.safer-community.net and let us know via our suggestions box.

■ The above information is from a leaflet produced by Crime Concern with funding from Gala Leisure. Visit Crime Concern's web site at www.crimeconcern.org.uk

© Crime Concern/Gala Leisure

Families to get involved in preventing crime

Children at high risk of getting into crime will be targeted and their families involved in steering them away from this path, thanks to over £1.36 million awarded to the Youth Justice Board by the Government's Invest to Save Budget.

The funding will allow five areas to pilot new family group conferencing programmes, run in conjunction with established schemes to prevent children becoming involved in crime. The family group conferencing schemes will be linked to Youth Inclusion and Support Panels (YISPs), which were set up in 2003 to prevent young people from becoming involved in crime. YISPs are voluntary schemes that target children aged 8-13 identified as being at high risk of offending.

This new money will enable existing YISPs to increase the involvement of children and their families in the design and delivery of plans to reduce the chances of the young person getting caught up in crime.

Sir Charles Pollard, Acting Chair of the Youth Justice Board, said: 'Ensuring that children are prevented from offending at the earliest possible opportunity is a key priority for the Youth Justice Board and Youth Offending Teams. Family group conferencing is an important restorative justice technique to ensure that families understand the risks that their children might pose to themselves, others and the wider community. It encourages families to support their child, so that they are more likely to lead a law-abiding life.'

© Reproduced by kind permission of the Youth Justice Board for England and Wales

Restorative justice

Information from Mediation UK

Restorative Justice centres around hearing what harm a crime has caused, and finding the best way to address that harm. This may be done through a facilitated meeting or type of mediation, although it does not necessarily involve face-to-face meetings between the victim and offender.

The key participants in Restorative Justice are communities, victims and offenders, though the UK's criminal justice system is increasingly seeking to adopt restorative approaches to its work. (The criminal justice system is the way we deal with people accused of criminal offences, and often results in a court hearing.)

In broad terms, Restorative Justice practitioners include all those who are finding ways of supporting victims, enabling offenders to make amends and engaging communities in problem-solving crime reduction work. The three main models of Restorative Justice practised within the UK are:

- victim-offender mediation
- family group conferencing
- restorative conferencing.

Most restorative work involves processes of communication, and aims for outcomes that empower victims, offenders and the wider communities to which they both belong.

What Restorative Justice can achieve

Restorative Justice is a process whereby victims, offenders and communities are collectively involved in resolving how to deal with the aftermath of an offence and its implications for the future.

It is a complex process that is still developing. As a result, there are many different claims about what it can achieve, and a range of perspectives on the issues that it raises. In summary, a Restorative Justice approach may be able to:

- give the victim a voice and a chance to get answers to questions

Mediation UK

'Restorative Justice supports victims, offenders and communities in seeking to repair the harm caused by crime, with mediation a favoured approach.'
Mediation UK

- re-affirm that the victim is not seen to be at fault
- assist the emotional well-being of the victim
- give the offender a chance to explain what happened
- encourage the offender to assume responsibility for his/her own actions
- prove the level of remorse of an offender
- give the offender a chance to make reparation and the victim or community to receive such emotional or physical repair
- resolve any conflicts between the offender and his/her family
- improve understanding between individuals
- explore reasons for offending and how these might be tackled
- motivate the offender to end a cycle of offending
- provide community support for rehabilitation

- help reinstate the offender as a member of the community
- reassure the community about the supervision of those who have offended and who live in the community
- enable those who wish to put the offence behind them to do so and look to the future
- heal the community
- assist the community in learning about crime prevention
- make something positive out of a negative event.

Restorative Justice within the criminal justice system

Mediation UK has campaigned for Restorative Justice to play a role within the UK's criminal justice system – the way we deal with people accused of criminal offences – and its use is now becoming increasingly widespread.

Although Restorative Justice is most often used as a complementary approach to formal legal processes, it can also work as an alternative. The UK's criminal justice system currently emphasises the reduction of re-offending, and only deals with those offenders that are prosecuted. It does not support the victims of the many crimes that do not go to court.

Restorative Justice enables victims to be heard and allows them to play an active role in the process of bringing offenders to justice. Additionally, it provides support for victims outside of the court system, regardless of whether a prosecution is brought or not. It achieves this through:

- victim-offender mediation
- family group conferencing
- enabling of reparation (often through community service orders)
- referring the offender to appropriate support services, such as drug rehabilitation units.

It is now generally accepted that Restorative Justice approaches can:

- avoid the victim feeling powerless and unheard
- minimise the offender's 'techniques of neutralisation' (where the offender is able to avoid acknowledging the real harm they have caused)
- minimise the misconceptions and fear of crime caused in communities by opening up discussions about it
- allow communities to take an active role in the prevention of crime.

Applications of Restorative Justice work in the UK

Restorative Justice programmes can be applied to all kinds of offence and all kinds of people. The only condition is that participants must want to take part and show an inclination to take the idea seriously. There are many ways in which such approaches are being used in the UK, the most common of which are listed below:

- Victim-offender mediation
- Family group conferences
- Restorative conferencing – used primarily in youth justice and other work with young people to try to resolve the problems that underlie truancy, exclusion, bullying and racial harassment
- Victim-offender groups – bringing together a number of offenders who have committed a similar type of offence (such as burglary, rape or robbery) for a facilitated meeting
- Conflict mediation services –

dealing with issues of custody and access to children in divorce proceedings

- Conflict resolution training programmes in schools – to help staff and pupils deal effectively with bullying and other problems
- Anger management programmes – used in work with prisoners, perpetrators of domestic violence and other groups prone to violence in the skills to handle problems more successfully.

Such programmes can operate independently of the criminal justice process – as community programmes,

for example – or at any stage of the legal procedure:

- To aid prevention of crime
- Alongside or instead of prosecution
- In conjunction with a police caution (as in Caution Plus)
- In conjunction with a court appearance
- As part of a court sentence
- Post-sentence.

■ The above information is from Mediation UK's web site which can be found at www.mediationuk.org.uk Alternatively, see page 41 for their address details.

© Mediation UK 2004

Government crime reduction targets

Many public services have set targets relating to crime reduction. Some are Government targets; some are set by services locally. Either way, it's worth knowing what the targets are. That way you can ask how well your services are meeting these. Funding bids are likely to be strengthened by showing how these will help meet the set targets.

Burglary
- Reduce domestic burglary by 25% between 1998/99 and 2004/05
- Ensure that, by March 2005, no local authority area has a domestic burglary rate more than three times the national average.

Vehicle crime
- Reduce vehicle crime (thefts of and from vehicles) by 30% between 1998/99 and 2003/04.

Robbery
- Reduce robbery in our principal cities by 14% by 2005.

Fear of crime
- Ensure that, by March 2002, levels of worry about burglary, car crime and violence are lower than they were in 1998.

Crime detection
- Increase the number and proportion of recorded crimes for which an offender is brought to justice.

Health
- Reduce the difference between the proportion of looked-after children who have been cautioned or convicted and the proportion of children in the general population

Active communities
- Make substantial progress by 2004 towards achieving one million more people actively involved in their communities.

■ The above information is from a leaflet from Crime Concern's safer-community web site which can be found at www.safer-community.net

© Crime Concern

Action for prisoners' families

**Prisoners' families are our greatest hope of reducing crime.
So why are they being punished?**

Over 150,000 people are committed into custody each year. Many are first-time offenders and their families are devastated by their imprisonment. Yet only a tiny number of prisoners' families get any information or support and many are just passed from pillar to post. Why? Because, in our society's response to crime, they are simply ignored.

For the partner of someone in prison, the punishment is equally hard. After the shock of arrest and separation, comes the struggle to pay the bills and bring up a family alone. Parents of prisoners often blame themselves and suffer guilt and self-doubt. Families feel frightened, lonely and humiliated. Their needs are largely ignored and they feel unable to confide in anyone.

Yet prisoners are up to six times less likely to reoffend if they maintain strong family ties whilst in prison. To do this, and be able to rebuild their lives after imprisonment, they and their families need support.

Visiting prison

'Our Centre is one of the few places where prisoners' families are treated with respect and dignity. Today I comforted a mum who thought her son was suicidal.

Another mother said she couldn't have got through her visit without us.'
Kay Goss, Littlehey Prison
Visitors' Centre

Being searched and forced to wait for hours, often after a long journey, is distressing. Yet prison visits are vital if a family is to survive together. It is particularly important for children to see and feel loved by a parent in prison.

Visitors' Centres in prisons can help greatly, preparing visitors for what to expect and supporting them after a difficult visit. Yet barely half of all prisons in the UK have established Visitors' Centres and most prison resettlement and counselling programmes still exclude families.

We are pressing for a Visitors' Centre at every prison, up-to-date information for visitors, special provision for children, and family issues included in Prison Officer training.

The silent sentence

Nine-year-old Joe was at home when his dad was arrested. He shut himself in his room and cried for hours. His behaviour changed and he became very withdrawn, not wanting to talk to anyone or play with his friends. He burst into tears every time his dad was mentioned.

Today, over 125,000 children in England and Wales have a parent in prison. Their world has been turned upside down. They may have to move home and school, or even be taken into care. Many suffer bullying, fail at school and find their friends aren't allowed to play with them any more.

Yet there is no official system to support these innocent children. Teachers or social workers who could help are often unaware of the situation; families try to hide their secret.

'Dad might not have been at home with us but we did have a close relationship. Once he went to prison that was taken away from me.'

■ The above information is from Action for Prisoners' Families' web site: www.prisonersfamilies.org.uk

*© Action for Prisoners' Families –
The National Federation of Services
Supporting Families of Prisoners*

KEY FACTS

- From recorded crime figures for England and Wales, it is estimated that in 2001/02 there was a 2 per cent increase in the underlying crime trend compared with the previous year. (p. 1)

- Crime in Scotland showed little overall change between 2000 and 2001, with a total of 421,000 crimes recorded by the police. (p. 1)

- The *British Crime Survey* estimated that just over 13 million crimes occurred in England and Wales, based on interviews taking place in the 2001/02 financial year. (p. 1)

- Theft (including vehicle and other household theft, but not including burglary) comprised almost half of all *British Crime Survey* crime in the 12 months prior to interview in 2001/02. (p. 1)

- The number of violent crimes reported in Britain during the third quarter of 2003 rose 14% compared with the same period the previous year. (p. 3)

- The historical trends in gun crimes are disturbing. In 1991, guns accounted for around eight per cent of homicides – 50 out of 623. In the year to April 2002, around 11.5 per cent of victims died from firearms – 96 out of 832. (p. 4)

- On one day in September 2003, 66,000 incidents of rowdiness, intimidation, littering, drunkenness, drug-taking and vandalism were reported to various public agencies – more than one every two seconds. (p. 5)

- According to Home Office Recorded Crime Statistics there were 5.2 million offences recorded in the year ending March 2001, down 2.5% per cent on the previous 12 months. (p. 6)

- One in four young people aged 12 to 16 has been a victim of crime in the last year, according to research published by Victim Support in 2003. (p. 7)

- One in three prisoners will lose their house while in prison; two out of three will lose their job, and nearly half will lose contact with their family. (p. 8)

- More than half of prisoners will commit another crime within 2 years of leaving prison. For men between the ages of 18 and 20 the rate is even higher. (p. 8)

- More than one in four of all teenagers – about 1.25 million of all young people – have committed a criminal offence in the last 12 months. (p. 13)

- A third (32%) of boys in mainstream education have committed an offence, compared with 20% of girls. (p. 15)

- Eighty-five per cent of young people think crime is getting worse. This is not surprising when you learn that two-thirds of young people have either been victims of crime or know someone who has. (p. 18)

- On 30 January 2004, there were 2,489 under-18-year-olds in prisons in England and Wales, almost exactly the same number as a year ago. (p. 23)

- The number of 15- to 17-year-olds in prison has nearly doubled over the last ten years. (p. 23)

- The overwhelming majority of the remanded young men are only held in prison for a short time and yet very little is done to address their problems. (p. 26)

- The age of criminal responsibility means the age at which a person can be prosecuted for a crime. It should be the age at which they understand the consequences of a crime and take full responsibility for that crime. (p. 29)

- Young people may be tried for a crime as young as 10, but the youth justice system means that in many ways they will be treated differently from an adult. So what are the differences? (p. 30)

- Police numbers in England and Wales have reached a new all-time high of 138,155 – and are rising at the rate of 6,000 every year. (p. 32)

- The latest Home Office figures for December 2003 published 2 March 2004 show that the number of police officers reached its highest level since records began in 1921. (p. 32)

- Restorative Justice centres around hearing what harm a crime has caused, and finding the best way to address that harm. This may be done through a facilitated meeting or type of mediation, although it does not necessarily involve face-to-face meetings between the victim and offender. (p. 37)

- Although Restorative Justice is most often used as a complementary approach to formal legal processes, it can also work as an alternative. (p. 37)

- Over 150,000 people are committed into custody each year. (p. 39)

- Today, over 125,000 children in England and Wales have a parent in prison. (p. 39)

ADDITIONAL RESOURCES

You might like to contact the following organisations for further information. Due to the increasing cost of postage, many organisations cannot respond to enquiries unless they receive a stamped, addressed envelope.

Action for Prisoners' Families
River Bank House
Putney Bridge Approach
London, SW6 3JD
Tel: 020 7384 1987
Helpline 0808 8082003
E-mail: info@actionpf.org.uk
Web site:
www.prisonersfamilies.org.uk
Promotes the just treatment of prisoners' families by the prison system and society across the UK.

Centre for Crime and Justice Studies (CCJS)
School of Law, King's College
London
3rd Floor, 26-29 Drury Lane
London, WC2B 5RL
Tel: 020 7848 1688
Fax: 020 7848 1689
E-mail: ccjs.enq@kcl.ac.uk
Web site: www.kcl.ac.uk/ccjs
www.crimeinfo.org.uk
CCJS is a charity which aims to inform and educate about all aspects of crime and the criminal justice system from an objective standpoint, and in accordance with the Centre's values.

Crime Concern Trust
Beaver House
147-150 Victoria Road
Swindon
Wiltshire, SN1 3UY
Tel: 01793 863500
Fax: 01793 514 654
E-mail: info@crimeconcern.org.uk
Web site: www.crimeconcern.org.uk
Works with local partners to prevent crime and create safer communities.

Crimestoppers Trust
Appolo House
66a London Road
Morden
Surrey, SM4 5BE
Tel: 020 8254 3200
Fax: 020 8254 3201
E-mail: cst@crimestoppers-uk.org
Web site: www.crimestoppers-uk.org
Crimestoppers is the independent charity operating the freephone

0800 555 111 helping to prevent and solve crimes.

The Howard League for Penal Reform
1 Ardleigh Road
London, N1 4HS
Tel: 020 7249 7373
Fax: 020 7249 7788
E-mail:
howardleague@ukonline.co.uk
Web site: www.howardleague.org
Works for humane and rational reform of the penal system. .

Mediation UK
Alexander House
Telephone Avenue
Bristol, BS1 4BS
Tel: 0117 904 6661
Fax: 0117 904 3331
E-mail:
enquiry@mediationuk.org.uk
Web site: www.mediationuk.org.uk
Mediation UK is a national voluntary organisation dedicated to developing constructive means of resolving conflicts in communities.

National Neighbourhood Watch Association®
18 Buckingham Gate
London, SW1E 6LB
Tel: 020 7963 0160
E-mail:
info@neighbourhoodwatch.net
Web site:
www.neighbourhoodwatch.net
National Neighbourhood Watch Association® was formed in 1995 to promote, support and represent the Neighbourhood Watch movement. It has now adopted as its mission statement: 'To make Neighbourhood Watch a Centre of Excellence for Community Safety.'

The National Youth Agency (NYA)
17-23 Albion Street
Leicester, LE1 6GD
Tel: 0116 285 3700
Fax: 0116 285 3777
E-mail: nya@nya.org.uk
Web site: www.nya.org.uk

www.youthinformation.com
Aims to advance youth work to promote young people's personal and social development, and their voice, influence and place in society.

Prison Reform Trust
The Old Trading House, 2nd Floor
15 Northburgh Street
London, EC1V 0JR
Tel: 020 7251 5070
Fax: 020 7251 5076
E-mail:
prt@prisonreformtrust.org.uk
Web site:
www.prisonreformtrust.org.uk
Aims at creating a just, humane and effective penal system.

Victim Support
Cranmer House
39 Brixton Road
London, SW9 6DZ
Tel: 020 7735 9166
Fax: 020 7582 5712
E-mail: info@victimcupport.org.uk
Web site: www.victimsupport.com
Victim Support is the independent charity which helps people cope with the effects of crime.

YoungMinds
102-108 Clerkenwell Road
London, EC1M 5SA
Tel: 020 7336 8445
Fax: 020 7336 8446
enquiries@youngminds.org.uk
Web site: www.youngminds.org.uk
YoungMinds is the national charity committed to improving the mental health of all children and young people.

Youth Justice Board for England and Wales
11 Carteret Street
London, SW1H 9DL
Tel: 020 7271 3033
Fax: 020 7271 3030
Web site: www.youth-justice-board.gov.uk
The aim of the Youth Justice Board is to prevent offending by children and young people.

ACKNOWLEDGEMENTS

The publisher is grateful for permission to reproduce the following material.

While every care has been taken to trace and acknowledge copyright, the publisher tenders its apology for any accidental infringement or where copyright has proved untraceable. The publisher would be pleased to come to a suitable arrangement in any such case with the rightful owner.

Chapter One: Overview

Crime and justice, © Crown copyright is reproduced with the permission of Her Majesty's Stationery Office, Recorded crime: by type of offence, 2001/02, © Crown copyright is reproduced with the permission of Her Majesty's Stationery Office, Surge in reports of violent crime, © Guardian Newspapers Limited 2004, Gun crime, © Telegraph Group Limited, London 2004, A day in the life of yob-culture Britain, © Telegraph Group Limited, London 2004, One day of anti-social behaviour, © Telegraph Group Limited, London 2004, How many victims?, © thesite.org.uk, Crime against young people, © Victim Support, Young victims of crime, © Victim Support, Crime and social exclusion, © Centre for Crime and Justice Studies (CCJS), Prison population, © Prison Reform Trust, Forecast prison population, © Prison Reform Trust, Sentenced population by offence type, © Prison Reform Trust, What's prison really like?, © HMP PARC.

Chapter Two: Young People and Crime

Through the eyes of children, © Children's Express, One in four teenagers commits a crime, © Guardian Newspapers Limited 2004, Young people and crime, © Youth Justice Board for England and Wales, Young victims of crime, © Victim Support, Under-16s experience of and attitudes to crime, © Crimestoppers, Focus on crime, © Norwich Union, Focus on crime – statistics, © Norwich Union, Better than cure?, © 2003 UK Youth, YIPs – a summary, © 2003 UK Youth, Young people in prison, © Prison Reform Trust, Youth sentences and penalties, © National Youth Agency (NYA), Busy doing nothing, © The Howard League for Penal Reform, Girls inside, © YoungMinds, Young offenders in prison, © Crown copyright is reproduced with the permission of Her Majesty's Stationery Office, Girls in prisons, © The Howard League for Penal Reform, Criminal responsibility, © Learnthings Ltd.

Chapter Three: Crime Prevention

Staying safe, © National Neighbourhood Watch Association®, Police numbers reach record, © Guardian Newspapers Limited 2004, Youth justice, © National Youth Agency (NYA), Alternatives to custody, © Centre for Crime and Justice Studies (CCJS), How to help tackle young people causing problems, © Crime Concern/Gala Leisure, Families to get involved in preventing crime, © Youth Justice Board for England and Wales, Restorative justice, © Mediation UK, Government crime reduction targets, © Crime Concern, Action for prisoners' families, © Action for Prisoners' Families.

Photographs and illustrations:

Pages 1, 17, 20, 30, 37: Simon Kneebone; pages 4, 25, 31: Pumpkin House; page 8: Don Hatcher; pages 11, 22, 35: Bev Aisbett; page 39: Angelo Madrid.

Craig Donnellan
Cambridge
April, 2004